CIT

T

Thomas Cook

WHAT'S IN YOUR GUIDEBOOK?

Independent authors Impartial up-to-date information from our travel experts who meticulously source local knowledge.

Experience Thomas Cook's 165 years in the travel industry and guidebook publishing enriches every word with expertise you can trust.

Travel know-how Contributions by thousands of staff around the globe, each one living and breathing travel.

Editors Travel-publishing professionals, pulling everything together to craft a perfect blend of words, pictures, maps and design.

You, the traveller We deliver a practical, no-nonsense approach to information, geared to how you really use it.

CITYSPOTS

TOKYO

Ryan Levitt

Thomas Cook

Written by Ryan Levitt
Original photography by Mark Bassett/The Source
Front cover photography (Sensō-ji) ©Jose Fuste Raga/Corbis
Series design based on an original concept by Studio 183 Limited

Produced by Cambridge Publishing Management Ltd
Project Editor: Catherine Burch
Layout: Donna Pedley
Maps: PCGraphics
Transport map: © Communicarta Limited

Published by Thomas Cook Publishing
A division of Thomas Cook Tour Operations Limited
Company Registration No. 1450464 England
PO Box 227, Coningsby Road
Peterborough PE3 8SB, United Kingdom
email: books@thomascook.com
www.thomascookpublishing.com
+ 44 (0) 1733 416477

ISBN: 978-1-84157-826-2

Project Editor: Kelly Anne Pipes
Production/DTP: Steven Collins

Printed and bound in Spain by GraphyCems

CONTENTS

SYMBOLS KEY

The following symbols are used throughout this book:

ⓐ address ⓣ telephone ⓦ website address
ⓛ opening times ⓟ public transport connections ⓘ important

The following symbols are used on the maps:

i information office	O city
airport	O large town
hospital	o small town
police station	motorway
railway station	main road
M metro and JR Rail	minor road
	railway

❶ numbers denote featured cafés & restaurants

Hotels and restaurants are graded by approximate price as follows:

£ budget **££** mid-range **£££** expensive

See all of Tokyo on a pedestrian crossing – Hachiko crossing

INTRODUCING Tokyo

Introduction

Tokyo is a dichotomy of old and new. It is thousands of years of history and the world of tomorrow wrapped up into one delicious sushi roll. Only on the streets of this neon-glowing metropolis will you see a woman dressed in a traditional kimono hail a taxi, or a shaven-headed monk as he chats on his mobile.

The buzz of Tokyo is electric. London claims to lead fashion trends, but Tokyo is where the unwearable becomes an everyday outfit. New York says it's the city that never sleeps. Wander to the neighbourhoods of Shinjuku or Roppongi after dark to see what partying all night really looks like.

And yet, Tokyo still has a past and a wealth of history to draw from. While it is one of Japan's newest cities (having only been transformed from a tiny fishing village to the site of the Imperial Court in the early 17th century), it has grown up fast – and no number of riots, earthquakes, wars, fires or rebellions have been able to slow down its progress.

Tokyo is all about combining big sights and spectacular sounds with moments of calm and contemplation. For every large museum and department store you enter there is a private garden or secret shrine. Addresses are almost impossible to understand, so don't even bother trying. Instead, get lost within the winding alleys and lanes that make up the Japanese capital to explore what this city is all about.

Many think Tokyo is not a city for those on a budget, but this fact is actually fiction. A few yen may make life easier, but Tokyo's greatest experiences come from the hearts of its residents. Be wowed by the wonder of it all or embrace a bit of Zen. No matter what your mind, body or soul is craving, Tokyo is sure to fit the bill.

Few people now wear a kimono on a daily basis

When to go

Tokyo offers great holiday options throughout the year. Festivals rage in spring and autumn, winter brings with it clear skies and great skiing just out of town, while summer's humidity is battled by music festivals and street parties.

Hotel rates are high throughout the year, but literally price themselves into the sky during the cherry blossom viewing period and the national holiday week known as Golden Week. New Year is another expensive period, as most of the nation is given the first week of the year off. The difference in price between a 3-star and 5-star hotel is steep, so be prepared to shop around during these periods.

SEASONS & CLIMATE

For the holiday of a lifetime, the best periods to visit Tokyo are in the spring and autumn. The sky is clear and bright during both these seasons and the temperature is temperate. May is an especially beautiful month, as the thermometer reaches an average temperature of 22°C (72°F) with light winds coming off the bay during warm days.

The rainy season hits Tokyo in June, with the next three months often turning into a humid, grey mush of wetness and sweat. Walking around Tokyo during the summer can sometimes feel like you are wading through a bath; it is, however, the best season to contemplate a trek up Fuji-san (Mount Fuji). If you find yourself feeling clammy, hop over to your nearest *onsen* (bath) to cool off, calm down and contemplate a little local tradition.

Winter is clear and cold. Snowstorms are rare but do happen, and the city copes well with ice and snow. Go directly to one of the public parks following a snowfall if you want to see an inspiring sight. A Japanese garden was made for a light dusting of snow. The pure whiteness seems to add an additional touch of beauty to an already inspiring layout.

If you hit the rainy season, don't let it dampen your spirits

ANNUAL EVENTS

There's always something to do in Tokyo. After all, as one of the world's largest cities, you have to keep the population entertained for at least some of the time. For a full listing of dates and activities, check out the website for the Tokyo Convention & Visitor's Bureau on www.tcvb.or.jp

April/May

Meiji Jingu Spring Festival The best time to see all of Japan's traditional entertainments in one place at the Meiji Shrine. See examples of *Noh* drama, listen to ancient court music and watch Edo-era dances being performed.

May

Sanja Matsuri (Festival of Asakusa shrine) The biggest Shinto festival in town is held the third weekend in May in Asakusa. Almost two million pack into the district to honour the founders of the Asakusa shrine, culminating in a large and colourful parade.

August

Obon Sort of like a Buddhist Hallowe'en, Obon is the day on which the souls of the dead are returned to the land of the living. Celebrants greet them with dances, fires and festivals.

September

Tokyo Game Show The world's largest video game showcase hits town. Geeks everywhere rejoice www.cesa.or.jp

October/November

Tokyo Motor Show Annual car show profiling the latest technologies and models. A must for grease monkeys and auto-freaks Ⓦ www.tokyo-motorshow.com

! When public holidays fall on a Sunday, a day off is given to make up for it on Monday, so be aware that all shops, public and financial institutions will be shut. Saturdays are considered a working day.

PUBLIC HOLIDAYS

New Year's Day 1 January
Coming of Age Day 2nd Mon in January
National Foundation Day 11 February
Vernal Equinox Day Varies: near 21 March
Greenery Day 29 April
Golden Week 29 April–5 May
Constitution Day 3 May
Children's Day 5 May
Marine Day 20 July
Respect for the Aged Day 15 September
Autumnal Equinox Day Varies: near 23 September
Sports Day 2nd Mon in October
Culture Day 3 November
Labour Thanksgiving Day 23 November
Emperor's Birthday 23 December
New Year 28 December–4 January

Cherry blossom viewing

The annual blossoming of cherry trees is an event beyond compare in this nation of seemingly conservative residents. During this period in early spring, an almost feverish pitch hits locals as they battle it out to stake their claim on the best patch of grass from which to view the delicate blossoms.

You might think that a naturally inspired event such as this would be a calm affair, but you'd be wrong. The cherry blossom season is front-page news every year with entire television shows dedicated to 'Cherry watch' segments as the season begins.

Spottings start in the south of the country as the weather heats up and slowly make their way to the capital. By the time blossoms finally arrive in Tokyo, the anticipation has been building for weeks and locals let out a collective sigh in relief.

The bulk of the action happens in Ueno Koen (Ueno Park). This is where half of Tokyo congregates to admire the views. Spontaneous parties are the norm, with much alcohol consumed and picnics enjoyed. While the beauty is a bit marred by the volume of humanity enjoying it, you can't help but admire the beautiful blossoms as they dance in the breeze.

Many commentators remark that the reason behind all the celebration and drunken antics is due to the lack of a traditional *carnival* in Japanese society. Cherry blossom viewing gives the Japanese an excuse to remove all class divisions and kick up their heels. The fact that it occurs just as the weather is warming up and spring hormones kick in is almost certainly an additional factor. Only in Japan can nature be the cause for such celebration.

The cherry blossom viewing dates vary each year according to the weather. However, the first sightings usually occur in late March or early April.

Cherry blossom – a quintessential image of Japanese beauty

History

While evidence of human settlements dating back to the Jomon period (10000 to 3000 BC) have been found, it wasn't until the 16th century that the spotlight shone on the town of Edo (as Tokyo was then known).

Provincial warrior clans tore Japan apart for much of the 15th century, eventually resulting in the rise of Tokugawa Ieyasu to the post of shogun in 1600. Ieyasu chose Edo as his base, and so it became the new capital following his ultimate victory.

Edo thrived until 1657, when a devastating fire destroyed much of the city. More than 100,000 people were killed during the three-day blaze. The redevelopment of the city transformed Edo as streets were widened and bridges introduced to encourage an easier flow of traffic.

Edo continued its hold on power during the next two centuries, enduring numerous floods and famines along the way.

In 1853, Admiral Perry's black ships arrived and Japan was forced to face the reality of a Western presence for the first time since white traders had been banned from the nation in 1639. The next two decades proved challenging for the nation as a massive earthquake in 1855 and the overthrow of the shogunate in 1868 created hardship for Edo's citizens.

When Emperor Meiji came to power, Edo was renamed Tokyo (Eastern Capital) and quickly became one of the most important cities in the world. Japan embarked on a rapid course of empire-building during this period, entering a series of wars that resulted in land grabs of Taiwan, Manchuria and Korea. The devastating Great Kanto earthquake in 1923 destroyed much of the city, but progress was unstoppable by this point and Tokyo was rapidly rebuilt despite the death of 140,000 citizens.

In 1941, the attack on Pearl Harbour brought Japan into World War II. The country's involvement ended in 1945, following the dropping of atomic bombs on Hiroshima and Nagasaki. Incendiary bombing became an almost daily occurrence during the final year of the war, with Tokyo facing the bulk of fire.

Occupation by US forces lasted seven years, with rebuilding taking place at a feverish place. The nation displayed its rebuilt pride to the world in 1964 when it became the home of the Summer Olympics.

Tokyo's economy exploded for the next three decades, finally ending with the collapse of the bubble economy in 1990. Today, the city continues to buzz – albeit at a slightly less frenetic pace than during the 1970s and 80s.

The Imperial Palace is the residence of Japan's Imperial family

Lifestyle

Go, go, go – that's what life is like in Tokyo. In this town, people are busier, cars move faster, shoppers spend more and trains travel more speedily than in any other city in the world. So how do the Japanese live at this pace?

Religion, while not as in-your-face as other parts of the planet, remains an important aspect of Japanese society. Shinto and Buddhism are the two main religions practised in the country – both performed as part of everyday life rather than as a Sunday ritual. A stop at a shrine or temple is a regular occurrence, but there is no set day on which practitioners must

Parks and gardens provide a place to slow down the frenetic pace of life

go. Instead, locals treat a trip to a shrine as a chance to slow down and contemplate life.

Gardens are another way to help locals slow down. The goal of a garden in Japan is to assist in the contemplation of nature and its relationship to the soul. Pebbles are scattered in water-features. Paths are orderly and manicured. Benches and seats provide locations from which you can absorb the simplicity and Zen-like aura. Western gardens would never work in Japan because they focus on colour and bloom. While the Japanese can appreciate the beauty of such a garden, the riot of colours and scents would not help them in terms of coping with the everyday stresses and strains of life in Tokyo.

Because there is such limited space in Japan, land is at a premium. Most young people stay with their parents until they marry; many even remain after that date. Property is extortionately expensive and mortgages can be 100 years in length. Apartment living is the norm with families forced to use one space as a dining room, TV room and bedroom.

DEFERENCE TO ELDERS

This is a must, especially when different generations occupy the same living space. For it to work, this close proximity requires strict codes of honour. This is reflected throughout society because the elderly are considered the most important members of a community due to their knowledge, skill and life experience. Therefore, if you see a senior citizen get on the metro, offer your seat unless you want to be considered rude.

Culture

TRADITIONAL

Visitors to Japan often state that an experience at a *Kabuki* or *Noh* theatrical performance was the highlight of their stay – but it's not for everyone. *Noh* is Japan's oldest theatre form and is highly ritualistic in structure and display. The central character always wears a mask and every performance is divided into five scenes. While dancing and war scenes are common, movements are often very slow. All *Noh* plays are intended to teach viewers about Buddhist thought and its benefits.

Much more accessible is *Kabuki* – a theatrical form that involves bright costumes, dances and interesting storylines. All performers on stage are male, including the beautiful female characters who act as symbols of idealised woman.

Bunraku is another popular form of theatre, this time using puppets. Challenging to operate (to say the least), Bunraku puppets take years of training to master. Most chief puppeteers spend two decades practising the arms and legs before they are permitted to work facial expressions. Bunraku performances may not be suitable for children, as they are highly stylised and can be extremely long.

If you want to explore traditional cultural experiences, two options to consider are tea ceremony and flower arranging lessons. A Japanese tea ceremony is highly ritualistic and is considered a necessary skill that must be learned by every citizen. Every movement has a meaning, and there are strict rules that dictate who will be served first, what side of the cup must face them, what actions you do and where you look.

Ikebana (flower arranging) is another art form that follows strict rules. Focus is placed on the linear arrangement of every aspect of the display, including the vase, shape of the flower, stems, leaves and branches. Many shops and cultural centres offer lessons in both tea ceremony practices and ikebana at regular intervals.

Noh, *Japan's traditional theatre, is highly ritualistic*

The weekend sees Harajuku teenagers throw off their conservative life

MODERN POP

The Japanese love pop culture and will buy anything thought of as cute at every opportunity. For many, kitsch and comics are a form of expression that is permitted in a society that frowns on going outside the norm. The Harajuku girls that congregate in the district at weekends are a prime example of this. They may look wild, but you'll find that the minute school starts on Monday, they'll be back to their conservative ways until next weekend arrives.

The Japanese love conformity. Most kitsch items will be small, hand-held and brightly coloured because they are easy to hide (in pockets) when situations need a more sombre tone. For the best examples of pop Japan, check out the boutiques of Harajuku and manga store in Akihabara.

View of the Tokyo Tower rising up over Tokyo

MAKING THE MOST OF Tokyo

Shopping

The Japanese love to shop – and when you experience the levels of service Tokyo shops provide, you'll understand why. Nowhere else in the world caters to shoppers as well as Tokyo. From the browsing experience to the moment of purchase itself, shoppers are treated like gold. And the immaculate gift wrapping is like a piece of art in itself.

For designer goods

Head to the streets of Aoyama or the department stores of Ginza to pick up the latest high-end goods. Many items are made specifically for the Japanese market, so if you spot something you like, buy it; you may not be able to purchase it outside Japan. Prices are on the high side. The only bargains you might find will be in boutiques that specialise in Japanese big names such as Issey Miyake or Comme des Garcons.

For street-style

Harajuku is where you'll find wild clothes and cutting-edge fashions. You might think some of the pieces look unwearable, but local teens will find a use for them somehow.

For electronics

Akihabara is the neighbourhood of choice for electronics. Discounts won't be found, but the wealth of goods is impressive. Many items here may not hit Western markets for years to come.

Prada – if you like shopping, you'll think you're in heaven in Tokyo

For pearls

The pearl industry is headquartered in Japan and you may be able to find top quality examples at prices less than you might encounter back home. For the finest examples, head to Mikimoto in Ginza.

For souvenirs

All the department stores in Ginza have a souvenir department. The best one-stop shop, however, is Oriental Bazaar. A boutique is located at Narita Airport for any last-minute purchases you might need to make.

Busy traffic in the Ginza district

Eating & drinking

Dining out is not something most Japanese families do. There are many reasons for this – cultural and economical – but that doesn't mean there's a lack of gorgeous restaurants to choose from. On the contrary, it is the business community that keeps eateries alive in this town.

In the Western world, it's all about going out for the multiple-drink business lunch. In Japan, though, daylight hours are a time for work. It isn't until the sun goes down that the expense account truly gets stretched.

If you aren't invited to a flashy dinner, then chances are you'll want to save money and savour local flavours. Noodle shops and quick sushi and tempura joints can always be found near station entries as they cater to the need of the anonymous salarymen who commute to and from Tokyo every day.

For ladies who lunch, Italian food is currently all the rage. Small cafés have now sprouted all over the shopping districts of Omotesando, Shinjuku, Harajuku and Shibuya. But this probably won't last long, just until the next ethnic fad takes over. Don't get too attached to a restaurant in these neighbourhoods, as it's likely to have disappeared by the time you return.

PRICE RATINGS

Price ratings in this book are based on the average price per course.

£ = up to ¥1,000 **££** = ¥1,000–¥3,000 **£££** = more than ¥3,000

Fast food

Typical Japanese fast food is the ramen noodle. Served in a soup broth with vegetables, seafood or grilled meat, it's a quick and filling way to sate your stomach. There will be a ramen stand or shop in every neighbourhood you visit in the city. Good places include under train tracks near major train stations and in the basement level of Ginza department stores. Not only will the food taste good, it'll also be the cheapest meal you enjoy during your stay.

Tempura tasty treats

Tempura

If you're a parent, then you'll be truly thankful for tempura. This tasty treat is a form of finger food that takes basic items such as shrimp and vegetables and coats them in a batter before lightly frying. Typically, you eat the items on a stick and dip them into a little sauce. Fussy eaters love it because it reminds them of French Fries or Onion Rings. Luckily, they taste much better than that.

Sushi

If you love sushi, then you'll be in heaven. Tokyo offers a plethora of top-notch sushi joints ranging from fine dining options to classic conveyor-belt style eateries. Those unfamiliar with sushi may have to get used to the fresh sensation of raw fish, but once you do the taste is beyond compare. For food that tastes like it just jumped out of the ocean, head to the streets around the Tsukiji fish market. From ship to mouth can sometimes happen in just a few minutes.

SPECIALISATION: LESS IS MORE

Unlike in the West, a restaurant in Japan will tend to specialise in one cooking style or dish. For example, you might find a sushi joint serving items made only from eel, or a tempura joint that exclusively dishes up shrimp items. Japanese restaurants specialise – often to such incredible detail that only a single item is on the menu.

Drinking

For Japanese businessmen, a boozy session late into the night is often a test of one's commitment to the company. Favourite tipples are local beer or the warm rice wine known as sake. Whisky is another favourite and is a common gift for executives. In the event that your head is pounding, wake yourself up at one of the numerous coffee shops all over the city.

A revolving sushi bar helps keeps your options open

Entertainment & nightlife

Tokyo is on the must-do concert schedule for most big-name acts in the world today – and that goes for musicians of all types. Pop, rock, jazz, classical, opera ... all the stars flock here, including many who you might have thought dropped out of the limelight years ago.

For years, Western music has dominated the cultural scene of the city. However, this is starting to change as new generations reappraise the sounds of Japan. Many of today's most popular local artists fuse traditional sounds into modern beats to create a hybrid that brings East and West together.

Don't forget – karaoke first began in Japan

For the widest variety of venues, head for Shinjuku

Classical music remains one of the most popular genres and there are more than just a few places in which you can hear it performed. During the boom years of the 1980s and early 90s, dozens of venues were constructed, but today's more frugal economy means that many of these performances are conducted to less-than-packed houses.

Despite this, Tokyo can easily lay claim to being the leading city in the world for classical enthusiasts, rivalling even Berlin in terms of musical quality and quantity. The main venues include the home of the NHK Symphony Orchestra at **NHK Hall** (ⓐ 2-2-1 Jinnan, Shibuya-ku ⓣ 03 3465 1751) and the Tokyo Symphony Orchestra based at **Suntory Hall** (ⓐ 1-13-1 Akasaka, Minato-ku ⓣ 03 3505 1101 ⓦ www.suntory.com).

Jazz is another popular genre with numerous clubs dotted around the entertainment districts of the city. Shinjuku offers the widest variety of venues, with everything from bebop to bossa nova on display. Most performers are local, so quality can vary. Many hotels feature jazz sets. While their musicians are often the best in the city, they can be a bit bland in terms of atmosphere. For top-notch acts and big names, the **Blue Note** (see page 100) is the club of choice. If you're a huge fan of jazz, try to plan your stay during the annual Tokyo Jazz Festival in August.

Pop and rock fans will be spoilt for choice – both with talented locals and huge international acts. The biggest (think Madonna and the Rolling Stones) will always be found at the **Tokyo Dome** (ⓐ 1-3 Suidobashi, Bunkyo-ku ⓣ 03 5800 9999 ⓦ www.tokyo-dome.co.jp/e/) – a horrible venue with lousy acoustics. Unfortunately, it's the only place in town large enough to meet demand.

Headliner acts in large music venues usually hit the stage at 19.00, meaning the performance will be complete early in the evening. On summer nights, it can feel decidedly weird to walk out of a sweaty venue after a killer gig only to witness the last rays of sunshine.

Glasto-fever has hit Japan recently with the latest cool trend being the weekend rock festival. The biggest of the bunch is the **Fuji Rock Festival** held every July (ⓦ www.fujirockfestival.com).

For teens and 20-somethings, dance music is the sound of choice. Japanese clubbers love their hard house and techno. Nowhere else will you hear fewer lyrics and sparser beats. Refreshingly, this is (mostly) done in a drug-free environment. If someone dances for hours on end, it is due to their devotion to the music rather than illicit substances. DJs such as the Chemical Brothers and Richie Hawtin consider Tokyo their second home.

Sport & relaxation

How do the Japanese stay so thin? It may have something to do with their diet – but that's not all that keeps locals going in this city of speed. Unlike other cities where the gym is the place to pump iron, Tokyo's residents largely stay away from such sweaty locations. This isn't due to a fear of bodybuilding, it's primarily about economics.

Space in Tokyo is at a premium and a good gym needs lots of it in order to accommodate equipment. Membership is very expensive, limiting the number of people who can afford to join. Instead, most locals keep active by taking advantage of the opportunities in public parks. Joggers, walkers and t'ai chi

The ancient tradition of Sumo wrestling

practitioners can all be seen throughout the day as they get their hearts pumping.

However, the leading sport practised by residents is martial arts. Several varieties are considered official forms of the sport, with judo, akido, karate and kendo the most popular. If you want to try it out or are an experienced practitioner, there are many dojo (martial arts gyms) that welcome foreign visitors.

Sumo wrestling, while less welcoming in terms of participation, is worth checking out as a spectator. At an initial glance, it may just look like a couple of obese men pushing each other to and fro, but it is actually a complex and ancient custom that can be gripping as you learn about it in greater detail. Its practice goes back more than two millennia and the rules are relatively simple. Basically, the goal is to push your opponent out of the ring or force him to touch the floor with something other than his feet. The biggest tournaments in Tokyo occur in January, May and September.

❶ An excellent way to immerse yourself in sumo culture is to attend one of the dedication ceremonies held at the Meiji shrine (see page 89) just before major events.

Accommodation

Space in Tokyo is at a premium, so don't expect a palatial suite when you check into your hotel – unless you spend a fortune. Budget travellers have plenty of options, depending on how intrepid they are prepared to be. For something quirky, why not try a capsule hotel? Designed for businesspeople who find themselves trapped in the city for the evening, each room, literally a capsule, comes complete with a television and simple mattress. If you are remotely claustrophobic, don't even think about trying them.

Better still, check into a *ryokan*. These guest houses are actually private homes usually decorated in traditional Japanese style. You will be expected to follow Japanese etiquette during your stay, which means removing your shoes before you enter the home and sleeping on a traditional futon.

HOTELS

Hilltop Hotel ££ Feeling creative? Then this is the place. The Hilltop Hotel is a hit with writers who come here to take

> **PRICE RATING**
> Hotels in Japan are graded according to a star system running from 1-star for a cheap *ryokan*, hostel or capsule hotel with shared facilities to 5-star for a luxurious property with numerous amenities. The ratings here are for a single night in a double or twin room.
> **£** = budget (under ¥10,000), **££** = moderate (¥10,001–¥30,000), **£££** = Expensive (over ¥30,000)

advantage of the antique writing desks and ionised air designed to help rid writer's block. ⓐ 1-1 Kanda-Surugadai, Chiyoda-ku ⓣ 03 3293 2311 ⓦ www.yamanoue-hotel.co.jp Ⓜ Metro: Ochanomizu

Hotel Yaesu Ryūmeikan £££ Location, location, location is what makes this hotel such a find. Just steps from Tokyo station, it offers simple rooms and complimentary Japanese breakfast. ⓐ 1-3-22 Yaesu, Chuo-ku ⓣ 03 3271 0977 ⓦ www.ryumeikan.co.jp Ⓜ Metro: Tokyo Station/Nihombashi

Hotel Okura £££ This fantastic hotel lacks the glitz of its newer rivals, yet continues to rank highly with visitors due to its high service levels. Opened in time for the 1964 Olympic Games, the main lobby has a cool kitsch factor and is a great place to unwind. There's even an onsite museum dedicated to Japanese porcelain. ⓐ 2-10-4 Tora-no-mon, Minato-ku ⓣ 03 3582 0111 ⓦ www.okura.com Ⓜ Metro: Kamiya-cho/Tora-no-mon

Mandarin Oriental £££ Speed 38 floors up to the main lobby and step out of the lift to be greeted by glass walls revealing the metropolis below. Rooms are some of the largest in the city. ⓐ 2-1-1 Nihonbashi Muromachi, Chuo-ku ⓣ 03 3270 8800 ⓦ www.mandarinoriental.com Ⓜ Metro: Mitsukoshimae

Park Hyatt Tokyo £££ Still one of the hottest places in town to rest your head, the home of *Lost in Translation* offers stunning views from its reception located on the 41st floor, large rooms and good-sized swimming pool. ⓐ 3-7-1-2 Nishi-Shinjuku, Shinjuku-ku ⓣ 03 5322 1234 ⓦ www.hyatt.com Ⓜ Metro: Shinjuku

Ryokans

Sakura Ryokan £ Traditional *ryokan* near the temples of Asakusa. Choose from Japanese and Western-style rooms. ⓐ 2-6-2 Iriya, Taito-ku ⓣ 03 3876 8118 ⓦ www.sakura-ryokan.com Ⓜ Metro: Iriya

Sawanoya Ryokan £ While it's not as conveniently located as other *ryokans*, this budget property is one of the friendliest in town. Book in advance, as it fills up fast. ⓐ 2-3-11 Yanaka, Taito-ku ⓣ 03 3822 2251 ⓦ www.sawanoya.com Ⓜ Metro: Nezu

A ryokan *room at Hotel Sawanoya*

Capsule hotels

Green Plaza Shinjuku £ Tokyo's largest capsule hotel is conveniently located just steps away from Shinjuku station. The 1 m x 2 m (3 ft x 6 ft) rooms have no doors, but they are comfortable and safe. Women are not permitted. ⓐ 1-29-3 Kabuki-cho ⓣ 03 3207 5411 Ⓜ Metro: Shinjuku

Central Land Shibuya £ Neither as large nor as recommended as the Green Plaza, this capsule hotel is good if you find yourself stranded in the region of Shibuya. Rooms fill fast, as it is one of the smallest capsule hotels in town. ⓐ 1-19-14 Dogenzaka, Shibuya-ku ⓣ 03 3464 1777 Ⓜ Metro: Shibuya

Capsule hotels – not for the claustrophobic!

Hostels

Tokyo International Youth Hostel £ Spotless shared rooms on offer. Night owls may be disappointed by the curfew which is strictly set at 23.00. ⓐ Central Plaza, 18th Floor, 1-1 Kaguragashi, Shinjuku-ku ⓣ 03 3235 1107 ⓦ www.tokyo.yh.jp Ⓜ Metro: Iidabashi

YMCA Asia Youth Centre £ Mixed sex accommodation. All rooms are private and simply furnished. ⓐ 2-5-5 Saragaku, Chiyoda-ku ⓣ 03 3233 0611 Ⓜ Metro: Suido-bashi

LOVE HOTELS

Due to the extortionate cost of property, many young adults live at home until a ripe old age. As courting couples find it challenging to get intimate when parents are in the next futon, the Japanese have created the concept of the love hotel. Dotted throughout the city, these properties can be rented by the night or by the hour. Ranging in quality from simple chambers to blow-out romantic venues complete with 'spewing' volcanoes, waterfalls and champagne glass-shaped bathtubs, the rooms are great for those looking for somewhere to stay that is quintessentially kitsch Japanese. In order to avoid embarrassment, many of the hotels are completely computerised. Look on the sign, choose a room that is lit up (anything unlit is occupied) and pop in your credit card or yen. Long-term stays are not possible, as these hotels will kick you out as soon as the sun comes up – so don't bring a suitcase.

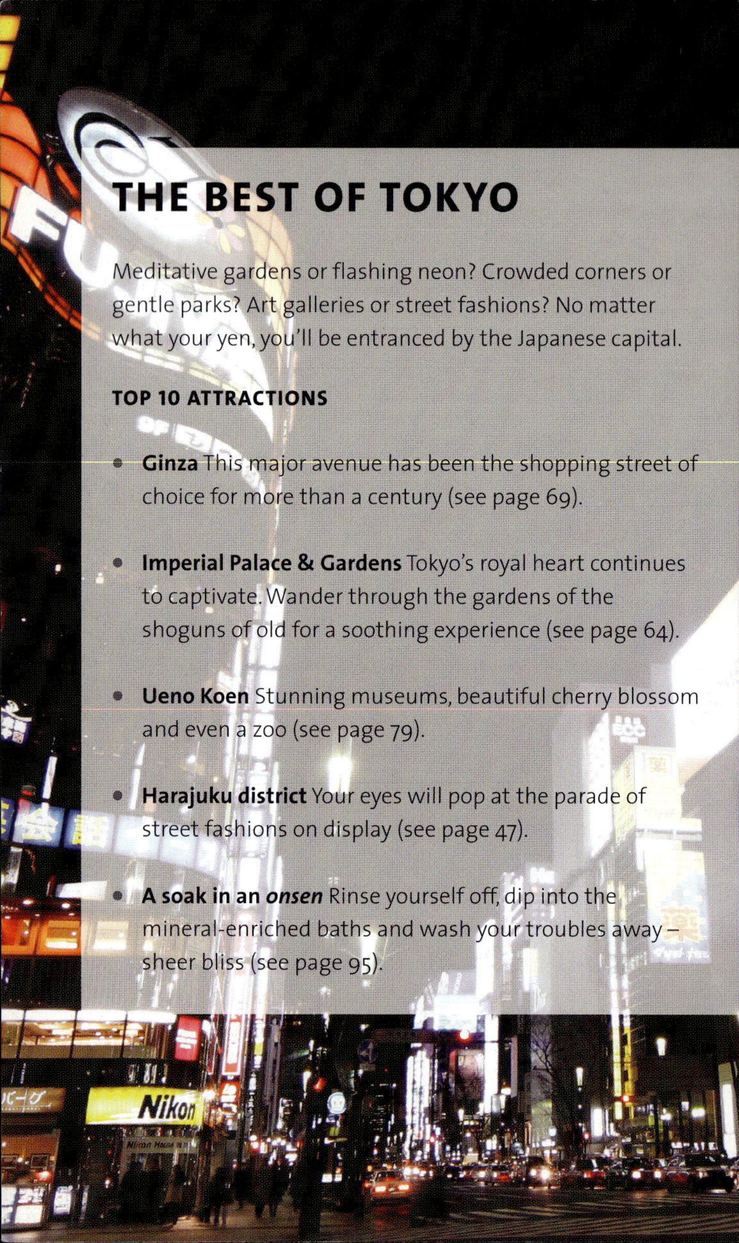

THE BEST OF TOKYO

Meditative gardens or flashing neon? Crowded corners or gentle parks? Art galleries or street fashions? No matter what your yen, you'll be entranced by the Japanese capital.

TOP 10 ATTRACTIONS

- **Ginza** This major avenue has been the shopping street of choice for more than a century (see page 69).
- **Imperial Palace & Gardens** Tokyo's royal heart continues to captivate. Wander through the gardens of the shoguns of old for a soothing experience (see page 64).
- **Ueno Koen** Stunning museums, beautiful cherry blossom and even a zoo (see page 79).
- **Harajuku district** Your eyes will pop at the parade of street fashions on display (see page 47).
- **A soak in an *onsen*** Rinse yourself off, dip into the mineral-enriched baths and wash your troubles away – sheer bliss (see page 95).

- **The Park Hyatt Hotel** Even if you aren't staying here, the Park Hyatt will inspire you to create your own version of *Lost in Translation* (see page 38).

- **Tsukiji market** The chaos of the auction; the buzz of the merchants – you'll have to wake up early but it's worth every yawn (see page 61).

- **Fuji-san (Mount Fuji)** Nature's most symmetrical volcano has been inspiring painters for centuries (see page 104).

- **Riding a *Shinkansen*** Fulfil your need for speed in one of the world's fastest trains (see page 129).

- **Kabuki-za** Witness this ancient art form and unmask the cultural traditions of Japan (see page 73).

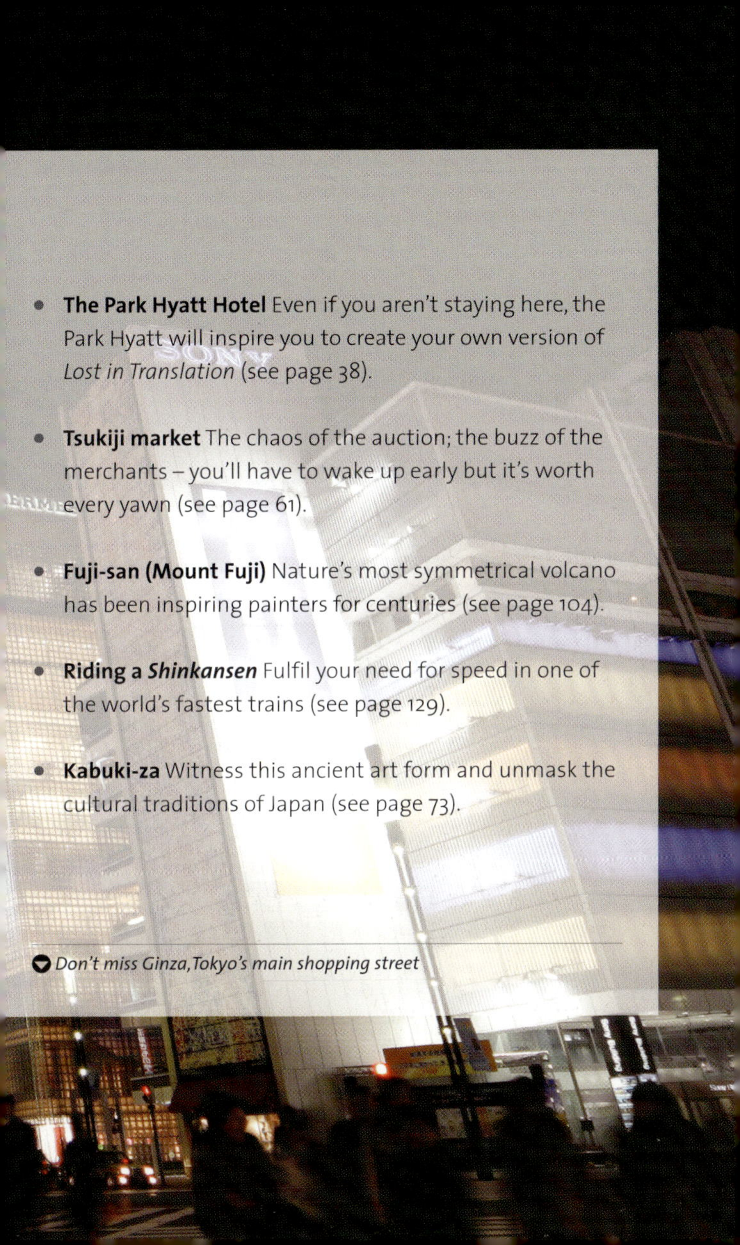

Don't miss Ginza, Tokyo's main shopping street

Whether you only have a few hours free in Tokyo, a few days or longer, here are some suggestions on how you can fill your time in Asia's wildest and most dynamic city.

HALF-DAY: TOKYO IN A HURRY

Spend an hour wandering through the Imperial Gardens to get in touch with your royal side. Follow this up with a walk down Ginza to pick up souvenirs and savour traditional levels of Japanese service. Every department store in town has a branch on this neon-covered stretch of pavement. Come prepared with comfortable shoes and a full wallet.

See the traditional side of Tokyo – the Imperial Palace

1 DAY: TIME TO SEE A LITTLE MORE

Continue your walk down Ginza until you reach Shinbashi. Take the metro line to Odaiba for a soak in a traditional *onsen* and a peak at the technologies of tomorrow. End the day with a ride on the Ferris wheel at Mega Web overlooking Tokyo Bay.

2–3 DAYS: SHORT CITY-BREAK

Spend a day shopping in Harajuku and Aoyama. Stick to Aoyama if high-end designer clothes are your style. Alternatively, weave your way through the alleys of Harajuku for funky street fashion. Head over to Shinjuku or Roppongi at night for fantastic clubbing and dining options. On Day 2, stick to the museums of Ueno and religious temples of Asakusa to bring a bit of calm and culture back into your frenetic visit.

LONGER: ENJOYING TOKYO TO THE FULL

Add a new dimension to your stay by getting out of town to Fuji-san (Mount Fuji), one of the world's most perfect-shaped volcanoes, and just a couple of hours away from Tokyo. Enjoy watersports and trail-walking, or challenge yourself by walking up the mountain. Time it right and you'll witness a spectacular sunrise. Add to the thrills by hitting Fujikyu Highlands, home to one of the world's fastest roller-coasters. On your way back, stop for a day in Yokohama, the often overlooked city across the Bay of Tokyo that is now Japan's second-largest metropolis.

Something for nothing

Tokyo has a reputation for being expensive, but there are still plenty of things to do if you are on a budget. One of the highlights is a wander through the Imperial Palace East Gardens. These meticulous gardens were once the private domain of the emperor and can now be appreciated by one and all for absolutely no charge.

Soak up the serenity of the temple in Asakusa

A stroll down the Ginza is a must for every tourist, if only to see the bright lights and big windows of the various department stores that call this street home. If you find yourself here during the lunch hour, head to the basement floor of the Hankyu Department Store where the cost of a delicious and filling bowl of ramen most certainly won't break the bank.

The serene Sensō-ji temple in Asakusa is an option if you want to connect with your spirituality. Legend says that the incense burned on the premises gives off a smoke that can cure visitors of many ailments – so make sure you waft the scent over you as you wander through the grounds.

For fashion inspiration, Harajuku is the place to go. The teens who congregate in this part of town wear anything and everything according to the trend of the moment. The parade of clothes is a sight in itself, especially on the pavement that leads from the station to Yoyogi Park. At weekends, you can even find Elvis impersonators swivelling their hips to the delight of the local populace.

There are plenty of buildings that offer incredible views of the city, but none better than in the Tokyo Metropolitan Government Building No. 1. There is no charge to enjoy either the north or south observation decks. However, the general rule of thumb is that the south observatory offers the best daytime views, while the north observatory inspires after the sun goes down. On clear days you can even see as far as Mount Fuji.

When it rains

Most foreigners tend to visit Tokyo during the summer holiday months. Unfortunately, this is also the time of year when humidity levels peak and the annual rains arrive. In the event that you find yourself under an umbrella, head directly to Ueno Koen, Tokyo's oldest public park.

If you only have time for one museum, make it the Tokyo National Museum

With its collection of world-class museums and galleries, Ueno Koen offers plenty of diversionary options when the weather turns foul. Make sure you visit the Tokyo National Museum – considered the world's finest collection of Asian Art – and the National Museum of Western Art with its strong focus on the French Impressionists.

Continue your cultural explorations by heading to Kabuki-za, the most accessible theatre offering traditional performances of *Kabuki* in the city. This highly stylised theatrical form isn't for everyone, so you can choose to witness a single act or a full five-hour production.

In the event your brain needs a break from all that art, then a trip to Odaiba might be just the ticket. Enter the world of tomorrow by visiting the showrooms of Toyota and Panasonic. Better still, go to the Museum of Emerging Technologies for a peak at what the lifestyle of the future may look like.

After you've immersed yourself in futuristic science, step into something more traditional by visiting the Odeo Onsen Monogatari hot springs. This beautiful *onsen* bath complex was constructed to resemble an Edo-era village. There are plenty of diversions to pass the time, including traditional games, food stands, massage chairs and, of course, the hot springs themselves. Open (almost) 24 hours a day, the complex is a perfect destination for those in need of a bit of relaxation. Grab a cotton kimono, rinse yourself off and sink into the sizzling waters. It may take a bit of time to get used to the heat, but your muscles will thank you for it.

On arrival

ARRIVING

By air

Travellers who fly to Tokyo will most likely land at Narita International Airport located 70 km (43 miles) away from the city. For details on how to get to and from the airport, see pages 128–9.

Narita International Airport t 04 76345000
w narita-airport.co.jp

ANA (All Nippon Airways) t 0870 837 8866
w www.anaskyweb.com
JAL (Japan Airlines) t 0845 774 7777 w www.uk.jal.com
British Airways t 0870 850 9850 w www.ba.com
Virgin Atlantic t 0870 380 2007 w www.virgin-atlantic.com

By rail

There are many train stations that service Tokyo from almost every corner of Japan. The main stop for the famous *Shinkansen* bullet trains is Tokyo station in the Marunouchi district. This is also the station that all coach and most airport train link services will bring you to. Other large depots include Shibuya, Shinjuku and Ueno stations. These stops service both long-distance and suburban lines. That said, they are more focused on commuter services and can therefore get packed during rush hours.

By bus/coach

Long-distance buses connect Tokyo with most other Japanese cities. Coach stations can usually be found outside the central train station of the city you are departing from.

By road

Most visitors to Tokyo do not drive. This is because the address system in the city is incomprehensible – even for locals. If you are driving somewhere, it is recommended that you get your destination to fax or send an English map so you can find out where to go. Street signs are also difficult to read and traffic levels – especially during rush hours – can be hellish. Taxis are extortionately expensive. If road travel is favoured, go by bus or long-distance coach.

The combined metro and JR rail system is fast and efficient

Metro Stop
Cathedral
Information
Police Station
Airport
Railway Stn
Hospital
N
TOSHIMA-KU
NAKANO-KU
SHINJUKU-KU
SUGINAMI-KU
SHIBUYA-KU
SETAGAYA-KU
YAMATE-DŌRI
SHIN-MEJIRO-DŌRI
MEJIRO-DŌRI
WASEDA-DŌRI
MEIJI-DŌRI
ŌKUBO DŌRI
ŌKUBO-DŌRI
SHOKUAN-DŌRI
OTAKIBASHI-DŌRI
ŌME-KAIDŌ
YASUKUNI-DŌRI
SHINJUKU-DŌRI
KŌSHŪ-KAIDŌ
HŌNAN-DŌRI
PATIO-DŌRI
NAKANO-DŌRI
SUIDO-DŌRO
EXPRESSWAY NO 4 SHINJUKUSEN
GAIEN-NISHI-DŌRI
INOKASHIRA-DŌRI
OMOTESANDO AVE
AOYAMA-DŌRI
EXPRESSWAY NO 3 SHIBUYASEN
YAMATE DŌRI
GAIEN-NISHI-DŌRI
Kanda River
Nakai
Ochiai
Takadanobaba
Waseda
Higashi-Nakano
Nakano
Shin-nakano
Nakano-Sakaue
Nishi-shinjuku
Ōkubo
Shin-ōkubo
Higashi-shinjuku
Wakamatsu-kawada
Ushigome-yanagi-ch
Seibu-shinjuku
Shinjuku-sanchōme
Akebonobashi
Nakano shinbashi
Nakano fujimi-chō
Nishi-shinjuku-gochōme
Tochōmae
Shinjuku
Shinjukugyoenmae
Yotsuyasanchōme
Yotsuya
Fire Museum
Minami-shinjuku
Yoyogi
Sendagaya
Shinanomachi
New National Theater Tokyo
Sangūbashi
National Stadium
Hatagaya
Sasazuka
Meiji Shrine & Inner Garden
Harajuku
Tokyo Hands Department Store
Aoyamaitchōme
Gaienmae
Meijijingūmae
Yoyogi-Uehara
Yoyogihachiman
Yoyogikōenmae
Higashi-kitazawa
NHK Broadcasting Center
Nogizaka
Omotesandō
Shin-daita
Shimo-kitazawa
Tobacco & Salt Museum
Tokyo University
Ikenoue
Komaba-tōdaimae
Shinsen
Shibuya
Setagaya-daita
Ikejiri-ōhashi
Hiroo
Gokoku

Tokyo
0 750 metres
0 750 yards
Hakusan
Myōgadani
Tōdai-mae
Nezu
Ueno-Kōen
Ueno
Iriya
KOTOTOI-DŌRI
SENKAVA-DŌRI
HAKUSAN-DŌRI
HONGŌ-DŌRI
KASUGA-DŌRI
BUNKYŌ-KU
Kasuga
Tokyo University
Okachimachi
Inari-chō
Tawaramachi
Asakusa
KAPPABASHI-DŌRI
KOKUSAI-DŌRI
EDO-DŌRI
EXPRESSWAY NO 5 IKEBUKURO ROSEN
Edogawabashi
Kōrakuen
Hongō-Sanchōme
Yushima
Shin-okachimachi
Tokyo Dome
Suidobashi
EXPRESSWAY NO 1 UENOSEN
Kagurazaka
Suehiro-chō
Kuramae
EXPRESSWAY NO 6
KYOSUMI-DŌRI
SOTOBORI-DŌRI
Iidabashi
OKUBO-DŌRI
IIDABASHI
WASEDA-DŌRI
EJIRO-DŌRI
Ushigome-kagurazaka
Kanda River
Ochanomizu
Akihabara
Asakusabashi
Ryōgoku
Shin-ochanomizu
Iwamoto-chō
Jinbō-chō
Awaji-chō
Kudanshita
Ichigaya
Hachiman-chō
YASUKUNI-DŌRI
Ogawamachi
Kanda
KANDAHEISEI-DŌRI
Narita International Airport
Kakagu Gijutsukan
INNER LOOP EXP
Kodenma-chō
Higashi-nihonbashi
Ichigaya
KANDA MINAMI
UCHIBORI-DŌRI
National Museum of Modern Art
CHŪŌ-DŌRI
Hama-chō
Morishita
KŌSOKUTOSHINKANJŌSEN
Kōjimachi
Hanzōmon
Fukiage Garden
Ōtemachi
Mitsukoshimae
NIHONBASHI-HONCHO
SHINJUKU-DŌRI
Imperial Palace
Tokyo
Suitengūmae
National Theater
Nijubashimae
Nihonbashi
Kiyosumi-shirakawa
Supreme Court
MARUNOUCHI
YAESU-DŌRI
Kayaba-chō
Nagata-chō
Sakuradamon
Yūraku-chō
Kyōbashi
Akasakamitsuke
Tokyo High Court
ATAGO-DŌRI
Hibiya
Takara-chō
Hatchōbori
EXPRESSWAY NO 9
SAGA
AKASAKA
Kokkaigijidomae
Ginza-itchōme
Hatchōbori
Akasaka
Kasumigaseki
SHŌWA-DŌRI
EITAI
Tameike-sannō
Ginza
Shintomi-chō
River
ROPPONGI-DŌRI
SAKURADA-DŌRI
Toranomon
Higashi-ginza
DŌRI
Etchūjima
Uchisaiwai-chō
Shinbashi
GINZA
KIYOSUMI-DŌRI
HIBIYA-DŌRI
Shinbashi
SHIN'OHASHI-DŌRI
Tsukiji
Roppongi-itchome
MINATO-KU
Tsukijishijō
CHŪŌ-KU
Sumida
Mercantile Marine University
HARUMI-DŌRI
Kamiya-chō
Shiodome
Tsukishima
Tokyo Tower
TSUKIJI
Roppongi
Onarimon
Tokyo Central Wholesale Market
PONGI
Zōjōji Temple
HANEDASEN
Daimon
Kachidoki
Azabujūban
Akabanebashi
EXP NO 1
EXP NO 2 MEGUROSEN
Shibakōen
Hamamatsuchō

TIME DIFFERENCES

Clocks are nine hours ahead of London (GMT). Daylight savings is not implemented but there is pressure to change that, so be on the lookout for alterations. In Tokyo at 12.00 noon, time at home is as follows:

Australia Eastern Standard Time 13.00, Central Standard Time 12.30, Western Standard Time 11.00
New Zealand 15.00
South Africa 05.00
UK and Republic of Ireland 03.00
US and Canada Newfoundland Time 23.30, Atlantic Canada Time 23.00, Eastern Standard Time 22.00, Central Time 21.00, Mountain Time 20.00, Pacific Time 19.00, Alaska 18.00 (previous day)

FINDING YOUR FEET

Tokyo is huge. In fact, it's one of the largest cities in the world (depending on how you measure size). Locating a street, let alone a neighbourhood, can be a challenge. The address system was created when Tokyo was still called Edo. Even locals have no idea how it works.

Street names don't exist. Instead, all addresses are based on numbers. The way it works is that Tokyo is divided into 23 districts known as *ku*. Inside these districts are smaller neighbourhoods known as *cho*. And then these neighbourhoods are divided even further into *chome*. An address will be written with three numbers which will tell you which *ku*, *cho* and *chome* it is located in. This will give you the general area you are heading for, but it won't get you to the exact point. To do this, either check out the website of your destination or ask them to fax a bilingual map.

ORIENTATION

Because Tokyo sprawls so much, it is hard to pinpoint exactly where the centre of town is. Traditionally, the Imperial Palace and Marunouchi have always been considered the heart of the city, but that all changed when the emperor lost his status as a living deity following World War II.

Ginza, located to the southeast of Marunouchi is the focal point for high street shopping. South of Ginza is a collection of islands recently developed to offer entertainment options and attractions. Here is where you will find a themed *onsen*, automobile and appliance showroom, shopping centre and amusement park.

Toyko Station in the Marunouchi district is the main intercity rail terminal

Toei Asakusa
Toei Mita
Toei Shinjuku
Toei Oedo
JR East Railways
Yurikamome
Wakoshi
Hikawadai
Hanno
Kotake-Mukaihara
Nishi-Takashimadaira
Shin-Itabashi
Nishi-Sugamo
Senkawa
Ikebukuro
Kanamecho
Otsuka
Sugamo
Mejiro
Mitaka
Ochiai
Takadanobaba
Shin-Otsuka
Sengoku
Myogadani
Hakusan
Takaosanguchi
Shin-Okubo
Waseda
Higashi-Ikebukuro
Todaimae
Gokokuji
Korakuen
Hon-Koma-gome
Edogawabashi
Honancho
Ogikubo
Kagurazaka
Kasuga
Higashi-Shinjuku
Ushigome-Yanagicho
Nishi-Shinjuku
Suidobashi
Wakamatsu-Kawada
Ushigome-Kagurazaka
Iidabashi
Hikarigaoka
Shinjuku-Nishiguchi
Akebonobashi
Shinjuku
Kudanshita
Tochomae
Shinjuku-Sanchome
Ichigaya
Jimbocho
Hatsudai
Yoyogi
Shinjuku-Gyoenmae
Kojimachi
Hanzomon
Takebashi
Hashimoto
Yotsuya-Sanchome
Nijubashimae
Yotsuya
Nagatacho
Sakuradamon
Yurakucho
Sendagaya
Akasaka-Mitsuke
Kokkaigijidomae
Kokuritsu-Kyogijo
Shinanomachi
Kasumigaseki
Akasaka
Toranomon
Tameike-Sanno
Aoyama-Itchome
Uchisaiwaicho
Kamiyacho
Nogizaka
Onarimon
Meiji-Jingumae
Gaienmae
Roppongi-Itchome
Roppongi
Shibakoen
Yoyogi-Uehara
Yoyogi-koen
Harajuku
Omote-Sando
Azabu-Juban
Akabanebashi
Hiro-O
Mita
Shirokana-Takanawa
Sengakuji
Shiroganedai
Takanawadai
Shibuya
Osaki
to Sangenjaya
Ebisu
Gotanda
Chuo-Rinkan
Naka-Meguro
Meguro
Nishi-Magome

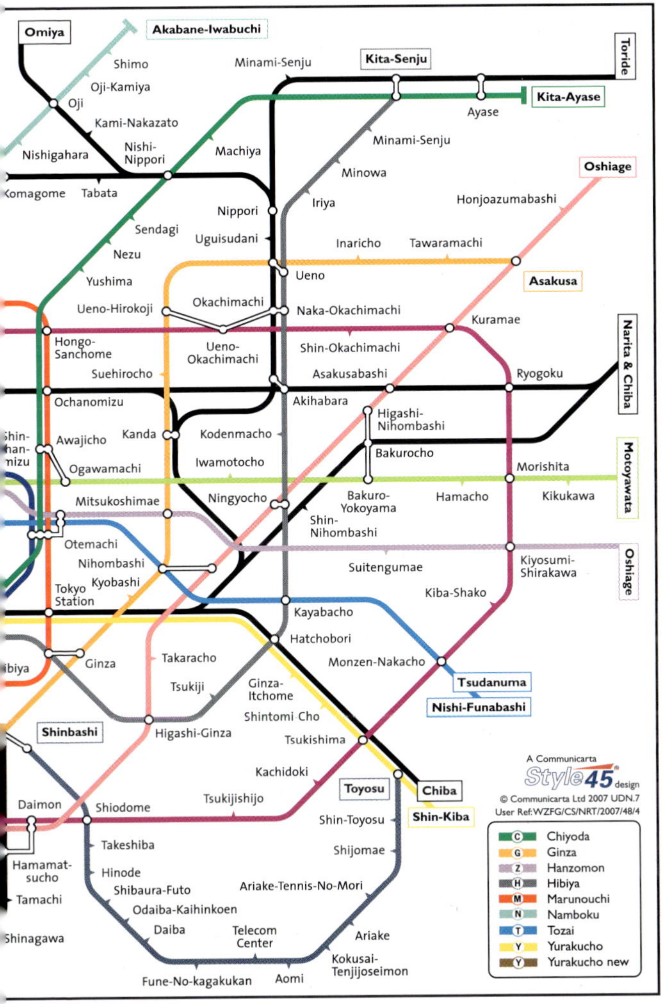

Omiya
Akabane-Iwabuchi
Shimo
Oji-Kamiya
Oji
Kami-Nakazato
Nishigahara
Nishi-Nippori
Komagome
Tabata
Minami-Senju
Kita-Senju
Toride
Kita-Ayase
Ayase
Machiya
Minami-Senju
Minowa
Oshiage
Honjoazumabashi
Iriya
Nippori
Uguisudani
Sendagi
Nezu
Yushima
Inaricho
Tawaramachi
Ueno
Asakusa
Okachimachi
Ueno-Hirokoji
Naka-Okachimachi
Kuramae
Narita & Chiba
Hongo-Sanchome
Ueno-Okachimachi
Shin-Okachimachi
Suehirocho
Asakusabashi
Ryogoku
Ochanomizu
Akihabara
Higashi-Nihombashi
Kanda
Kodenmacho
Shin-Ochanomizu
Awajicho
Bakurocho
Ogawamachi
Iwamotocho
Morishita
Motoyawata
Mitsukoshimae
Ningyocho
Bakuro-Yokoyama
Hamacho
Kikukawa
Shin-Nihombashi
Otemachi
Nihombashi
Suitengumae
Kiyosumi-Shirakawa
Oshiage
Tokyo Station
Kyobashi
Kiba-Shako
Kayabacho
Hatchobori
Hibiya
Ginza
Takaracho
Monzen-Nakacho
Tsudanuma
Tsukiji
Ginza-Itchome
Nishi-Funabashi
Shintomi Cho
Shinbashi
Higashi-Ginza
Tsukishima
Kachidoki
Toyosu
Chiba
Daimon
Shiodome
Tsukijishijo
Shin-Kiba
Shin-Toyosu
Hamamatsucho
Takeshiba
Shijomae
Hinode
Tamachi
Shibaura-Futo
Ariake-Tennis-No-Mori
Odaiba-Kaihinkoen
Shinagawa
Daiba
Telecom Center
Ariake
Kokusai-Tenjijoseimon
Fune-No-kagakukan
Aomi
A Communicarta Style45 design
© Communicarta Ltd 2007 UDN.7
User Ref: WZFG/CS/NRT/2007/48/4
C Chiyoda
G Ginza
Z Hanzomon
H Hibiya
M Marunouchi
N Namboku
T Tozai
Y Yurakucho
Y Yurakucho new

Go west from here to hit Roppongi, Tokyo's newest entertainment district, and then Shibuya, a district known for its vibrant pop culture, karaoke bars, nightclubs, music and manga cafés. From here, it's a quick hop north to Harajuku (for throwaway teen fashion) and then Aoyama (for designer shops).

Go north again to Shinjuku for hip nightlife, clubbing and more. Then take the train almost all the way back to Marunouchi in a clockwise direction to Ueno, for its street markets, shrines and park, or Asakusa for its temple and religious offerings.

Finally, one stop south is Akihabara. Geeks, computer whizzes and manga maniacs head straight to this area of glittering electronics to do their shopping.

GETTING AROUND

The combined metro and Japan Railways system is fast, efficient and goes pretty much everywhere in town. Many platform signs are only in Japanese. When in doubt, count the number of stations you travel to find your way to your destination.

Car hire

You will not need a car in Tokyo, as public transport is so efficient. The minimum age for renting an economy car is 25 and an international driving licence will be required. Car rental companies can be found at all major airports and train stations.

The view from Tokyo Tower which, at 333 m high, just beats the Eiffel Tower

THE CITY OF Tokyo

Central Tokyo: Marunouchi, Ginza & Tsukiji

While it would be hard to declare any neighbourhood in Tokyo the centre of the city due to the amount of sprawl, the historical heart of the capital lies in Marunouchi at the site of the Imperial Palace. Home to the emperor, the grounds are opened to the public on just two days a year. See page 64 for more details.

Further south is Ginza, a street synonymous with shopping since branches of the city's famous department stores opened to the public in the late 19th century. A stroll down the pavement is considered a local must-do. Weekend afternoons beckon the crowds as the multi-lane avenue is closed to car traffic in order to accommodate the numerous consumers.

Go closer to the bay in order to visit the Tsukiji fish market. Visitors will be in awe of the sheer volume of the place, which holds more than 60,000 people at its peak. The tuna auction is the main draw, but the cheap and fresh seafood restaurants are just as worthy of a visit.

SIGHTS & ATTRACTIONS

Hama-Rikyū Onshi Teien (Hama-Rikyu Detached Garden)
Formerly the private garden of an 18th-century shogun, this green space was transformed into a public park in 1945. Much of it remains prohibited due to its use as a nature reserve, but many of the original royal buildings are used for formal functions.

1-1 Hama-Rikyu Teien, Chuo-ku 03 3541 0200 09.00–17.00 Metro: Shiodome. Admission charge.

Tokyo Central Wholesale Market

Tokyo's fish market is a bustling hive of activity almost every day of the week. The market itself is huge – more than 54 acres, with over 15,000 people employed in every corner of the area. A highlight to any visit is the massive fish and seafood auction. Different varieties are sold at various hours of the day, but the biggest draw is always the tuna auction, which occurs 05.00–06.30.

When visiting, keep in mind that this is a place of business. If you get in the way of the traders they are liable to get very angry. Also, photos are forbidden during the auction. If you do attempt to take any, you will be ushered away from the area. Make sure you wear comfortable shoes and clothing that you don't mind getting dirty, as a constant flow of water and ice on the floor gets very slippery.

Tsukiji Market www.tsukiji-market.or.jp 05.00–12.00 (05.00–06.30 for tuna auction only) Mon–Sat, closed 2 Weds per month, all national holidays, and for a 2-wk period in August and at New Year Metro: Tsjukijishijo

CULTURE

ADMT Advertising Museum Tokyo

How are humans manipulated into prime consumers? This museum takes a look at advertising from the 17th century (when basic printing techniques were introduced) to today's

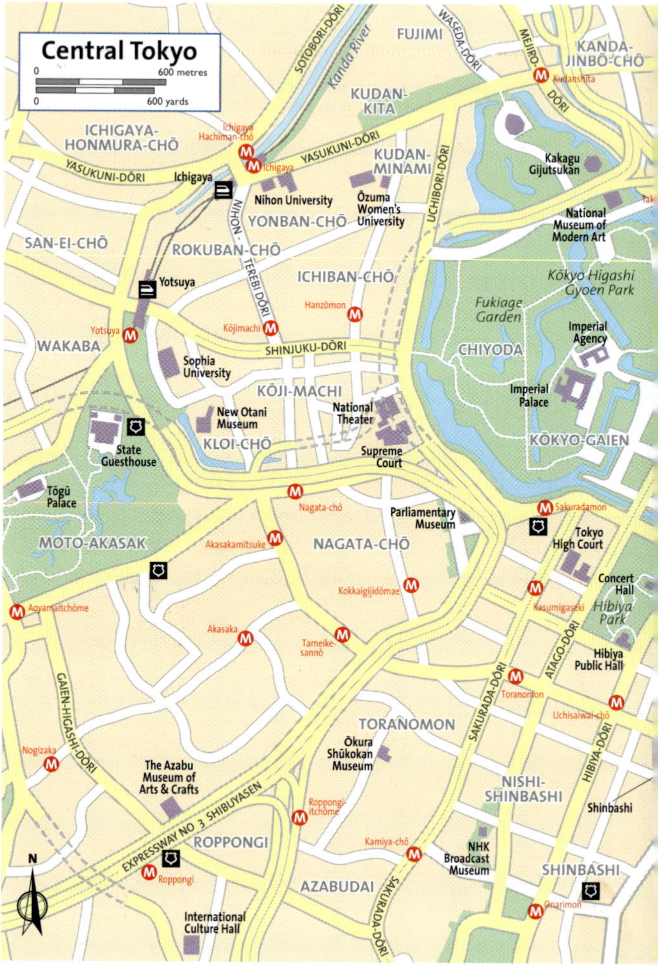
Central Tokyo
0
600 metres
0
600 yards
FUJIMI
KANDA-JINBŌ-CHŌ
Kudanshita
KUDAN-KITA
ICHIGAYA-HONMURA-CHŌ
Ichigaya Hachiman-chō
Ichigaya
YASUKUNI-DŌRI
KUDAN-MINAMI
Kakagu Gijutsukan
Nihon University
Ōzuma Women's University
YONBAN-CHŌ
National Museum of Modern Art
SAN-EI-CHŌ
ROKUBAN-CHŌ
Yotsuya
ICHIBAN-CHŌ
Kōkyo Higashi Gyoen Park
Fukiage Garden
Hanzōmon
Kōjimachi
Imperial Agency
WAKABA
SHINJUKU-DŌRI
CHIYODA
Sophia University
KŌJI-MACHI
Imperial Palace
New Otani Museum
National Theater
KLOI-CHŌ
State Guesthouse
Supreme Court
KŌKYO-GAIEN
Tōgū Palace
Nagata-chō
Parliamentary Museum
Sakuradamon
MOTO-AKASAK
Akasakamitsuke
NAGATA-CHŌ
Tokyo High Court
Concert Hall
Kokkaigijidōmae
Kasumigaseki
Hibiya Park
Aoyamaitchōme
Akasaka
Tameike-sannō
Hibiya Public Hall
Toranomon
Uchisaiwai-chō
TORANOMON
Ōkura Shūkokan Museum
Nogizaka
The Azabu Museum of Arts & Crafts
NISHI-SHINBASHI
Shinbashi
Roppongi-itchōme
ROPPONGI
Kamiya-chō
NHK Broadcast Museum
SHINBASHI
Roppongi
AZABUDAI
Onarimon
International Culture Hall
N
SOTOBORI-DŌRI
Kanda River
WASEDA-DŌRI
MEJIRO-DŌRI
UCHIBORI-DŌRI
NIHON-TEREBI DŌRI
GAIEN-HIGASHI-DŌRI
EXPRESSWAY NO 3 SHIBUYASEN
SAKURADA-DŌRI
ATAGO-DŌRI
HIBIYA-DŌRI

Nicolai Cathedral
Shin-ochanomizu
Ogawamachi
Awaji-chō
Transportation Museum
Akihabara
Iwamoto-chō
Asakusabashi
Ryoguko
EXPRESSWAY NO 6
YASUKUNI-DŌRI
Bakurochō
HIGASHI-NIHONBASHI
Higashi-nihonbashi
IWAMOTO-CHŌ
KANDA-OGAWA-MACHI
Kanda
KANDAHEISEI DŌRI
SOTOBORI-DŌRI
EXPRESSWAY NO 1 UENOSEN
Kodenma-chō
EDO-DŌRI
Bakuro-yokoyama
KIYOSUBASHI-DŌRI
CHŪŌ-DŌRI
LOOP EXP
ŌTE-MACHI
Shin-nihonbashi
Hama-chō
Communications Museum
Currency Museum
Ōtemachi
Mitsukoshimae
Ningyō-chō
NIHONBASHI-HAMA-CHO
KŌSOKUTOSHINKANJŌSEN
EITAI-DŌRI
SHIN'ŌHASHI DŌRI
HIBIYA-DŌRI
Kite Museum
Nihonbashi
Suitengūmae
EXPRESSWAY NO 7 KOMATSUGAWASEN
Tokyo
Nijubashimae
NIHONBASHI
MARUNOUCHI
Bridgestone Museum of Art
Kayaba-chō
EXPRESSWAY NO 9
Shinkansen
Idemitsu Museum of Art
KYŌBASHI
Kyōbashi
YAESU-DŌRI
Takara-chō
SAGA
Yūraku-chō
National Film Centre
Hatchōbori
KAJIBASHI-DŌRI
HATCHŌBORI
Shinhachobori
SHINKAWA
Ginza-itchōme
EITAI
SHINTOMI
IRIFUNE
Ginza
GINZA
SHIN'ŌHASHI-DŌRI
Shintomi-chō
Higashi-ginza
Kabukiza
TSUKUDA
Etchujima
AKASHI-CHŌ
Tsukiji
TSUKADA-ŌHASHI
Mercantile Marine University
KIYOSUMI-DŌRI
Tsukijishijo
HARUMI-DŌRI
Sumida River
Tsukishima
TSUKIJI
TSUKISHIMA
HANEDASEN
Hama-Rikyū Onshi Teien
Tokyo Central Wholesale Market
Kachidoki
Metro Stop
Cathedral
Information
Police Station
Airport
Railway Stn
Hospital

IMPERIAL PALACE & GARDENS

Before World War II, the Emperor of Japan ruled his country from the luxury and exclusivity of the Imperial Palace, separated from the city by an imposing moat and heavy stone walls. His godlike status was revoked at the end of

The closest you'll get to the Imperial Palace is the Nijubashi bridge

the war, yet the sense of power and privilege that emanates from this structure remains. Except for two days a year (2 January and the emperor's birthday on 23 December), the grounds are shut to the general public – and even then access is limited.

The palace that exists today is the second on these grounds. The original, Edo Castle, was constructed to meet the shogun's need for an impregnable location that could dazzle the masses. When it was completed in 1640, it was the largest castle in the world.

After taking the obligatory photo from Nijubashi (Double Bridge), most tourists head to Kokyo Higashi Gyoen (Imperial Palace East Gardens). Surviving buildings include the Hundred-Man Guardhouse, which housed four different shifts of 100 men employed to guard the castle complex, and a Tea Pavilion dating back to the early 19th century.

On the west side is a moat that houses a gaggle of graceful swans and a pathway that leads to the upper fortress known as Shio-mi-zaka.

Many locals visit the gardens for a spot of meditation and silence – difficult to find in this megalopolis of neon, traffic and crowds.

Ⓐ Chiyoda, Chiyoda-ku 🕒 09.00–16.30 Ⓜ Metro: Otemachi

subtle imagery employed in films, magazines and TV shows. Sometimes kitsch, it's always fascinating.
ⓐ Caretta Shiodome B1F-B2F, 1-8-2 Higashi-Shinbashi, Minato-ku ⓣ 03 6218 2500 ⓦ www.admt.jp ⓛ 11.00–18.30 Tues–Fri, 11.00–16.30 Sat ⓝ Metro: Shinbashi/Shiodome

Bridgestone Museum of Art

This collection, compiled by the Japanese founder of the Bridgestone Tire Company, boasts some of the finest examples of French Impressionist art in the country. Other highlights include Japanese paintings in Western styles, Old Masters and ancient sculpture.
ⓐ 1-10-1 Kyobashi, Chuo-ku ⓣ 03 3563 0241 ⓦ www.bridgestone-museum.gr.jp ⓛ 10.00–20.00 Tues–Sat, 10.00–18.00 Sun ⓝ Metro: Tokyo. Admission charge.

Communications Museum

Alexander Graham Bell would have loved this museum, which takes a look at the history of phone and post services in Japan. Stamp collectors will be drawn to the 280,000+ examples of stamps from every corner of the globe, while non-philatelists can examine the inner working of a phone and determine how a call actually works.
ⓐ 2-3-1 Otemachi, Chiyoda-ku ⓣ 03 3244 6811 ⓛ 09.00–16.30 Tues–Sun ⓝ Metro: Otemachi. Admission charge.

Currency Museum

Learn about the history of Japanese money at this museum with a heap of displays including 12th-century coins imported

from China and early yen from when the currency was introduced in the late 19th century.
ⓐ 1-3-1 Nihonbashi-Hongokucho, Chuo-ku ⓣ 03 3277 3037
ⓦ www.imes.boj.or.jp ◷ 09.30–16.30 Tues–Sun Ⓜ Metro: Mitsukoshimae

Idemitsu Museum of Art

Dedicated to the arts of East Asia, this museum is renowned for its superb collection of porcelains and ceramics from China and Japan. Other displays focus on Zen paintings, woodblock prints and calligraphy.
ⓐ Tei Geki Bldg 9F, 3-1-1 Marunouchi, Chiyoda-ku ⓣ 03 3213 9404
ⓦ www.idemitsu.co.jp/museum ◷ 10.00–17.00 Tues–Thur, Sat & Sun, 10.00–19.00 Fri Ⓜ Metro: Hibiya. Admission charge.

Kagaku Gijutsukan (Japan Science Foundation Science Museum)

One for the kids, this science museum tries to teach basic science lessons using interactive displays. While everything is in Japanese, you won't need to know any of the lingo in order to have fun trying out the games and activities.
ⓐ 2-1 Kitanomaru Koen, Chiyoda-ku ⓣ 03 3212 8544
ⓦ www.jsf.or.jp ◷ 09.30–16.50 Ⓜ Metro: Takebashi. Admission charge.

Kite Museum

The art of kite making is highly respected in Japan. This museum boasts examples from all over the country in almost every shape imaginable. Many use Japanese mythology for

inspiration. Children can enjoy taking part in a kite-making workshop if you call in advance.
ⓐ Taimeiken 5F, 1-12-10 Nihonbashi, Chuo-ku ⓣ 03 3275 2704 ⓦ www.tako.gr.jp ◷ 11.00–17.00 Mon–Sat Ⓜ Metro: Nihonbashi. Admission charge.

National Museum of Modern Art

Built in 1969, the National Museum of Modern Art focuses on contemporary Japanese works, with a major concentration on post-war paintings and sculptures. As the museum is situated next to the walls of the Imperial Palace, it's a convenient place to view the gardens, especially during cherry blossom season (see pages 14–15).

The Kite Museum. Japanese kites make great souvenirs

ⓐ 3-1 Kitanomaru Koen, Chiyoda-ku ⓣ 03 5777 8600
ⓦ www.momat.go.jp ⓒ 10.00–17.00 Tues–Thur, Sat & Sun, 10.00–20.00 Fri ⓝ Metro: Takebashi. Admission charge.

Transportation Museum

Originally a railway museum, modern additions include displays chronicling developments in air, space and automotive transportation methods. The train exhibits remain the highlight of the collection. Kids will love the interactive tasks that allow you to virtually drive a train through the streets of Tokyo.
ⓐ 1-25 Kanda-Sudacho, Chiyoda-ku ⓣ 03 3251 8481
ⓦ www.kouhaku.or.jp ⓒ 09.30–17.00 Tues–Sun
ⓝ Metro: Akihabara. Admission charge.

RETAIL THERAPY

Shopping streets & markets

Ginza is traditionally the main shopping street in Tokyo. It is home to the bulk of the city's major department stores, including Mitsukoshi – often thought to be the most prestigious of the lot. Ginza's reputation as a shopper's paradise began in 1872 following a devastating fire. A decision was made to rebuild the street in the Western style, complete with widened roads to accommodate horse traffic and gas lighting. It quickly became the fanciest spot in town. Many big names, such as the pearl manufacturer Mikimoto, all have flagships here and remain on the same spot as their original boutiques built in the late 19th century. Avoid the constant traffic and crowds on weekend afternoons between 12.00 and 17.00 when the street is closed to cars between Shinbashi and Kyo-bashi.

TAKING A BREAK

Naokyu £ ❶ Finding a cheap bite while shopping the Ginza can be a challenge – but one that Naokyu easily rectifies. Specialising in various types of ramen, this establishment is almost always full, especially during the lunch hours when the queue can be a block long. ⓐ Hankyu Department Store H2, 5-2-1 Ginza, Chuo-ku ⓣ 03 3571 0957 ⓛ 11.00–21.00 Mon–Sat, 11.00–20.00 Sun ⓜ Metro: Ginza

AFTER DARK

Restaurants

Edo-Gin £–££ ❷ The streets around the Tsukiji fish market are known for their incredible restaurants specialising in fresh sushi. Edo-Gin is one of the better options. Choose your meal from the fish tank in the centre of the room. From tank to stomach should only take a few minutes. The set lunch menu is very well priced for those on a budget. ⓐ 4-5-1 Tsukiji, Chuo-ku ⓣ 03 3543 4401 ⓛ 11.00–21.30 Mon–Sat, 11.30–21.00 Sun ⓜ Metro: Tsukiji

Kanda Yabu Soba ££ ❸ Outside Japan, a restaurant specialising in Japanese food will serve a wide cross-section of national dishes. Inside Japan, it's another story, with many establishments specialising in an individual menu item. In this restaurant's case, it is the soba noodle (a buckwheat noodle often served cold) that provides the focus. Almost all the main courses feature this item. Make the meal complete with sake

The fish market at Tsukiji is vast and very busy

and a variety of side dishes. ⓐ 2-10 Kanda-Awajicho, Chiyoda-ku ⓣ 03 3251 0287 ⓛ 11.30–20.00 Ⓜ Metro: Kanda

Botan £££ ❹ Chicken sukiyaki is the only thing served at this traditional eatery – but what a dish it is! The ladies who serve will cook the meal right in front of you in a large pot. Be marvelled by both the taste and the quaint surroundings. ⓐ 1-15 Kanda-Sudacho, Chiyoda-ku ⓣ 03 3251 0577 ⓛ 11.30–21.00 Mon–Sat Ⓜ Metro: Kanda

Rangetsu £££ ❺ In order to raise the Japanese speciality of Kobe beef, a head of cattle needs to be given a daily massage and fed a daily dose of beer. Sound pampered? It should be considering how much it costs. After all this luxury, the result is beef that is marbled throughout – perfect for a dish of sukiyaki or shabu-shabu. Expensive, but worth it if you like your meat rich and perfectly prepared. ⓐ 3-5-8 Ginza, Chuo-ku ⓣ 03 3567 1021 ⓛ 11.30–22.00 Ⓜ Metro: Ginza

Bars, clubs & discos

Kagaya Positively bizarre – these are the only adjectives that could be used to describe this kooky bar, considering the dressing-up antics of its owner. Be prepared to deal with a cocktail that explodes, hums or sings the Japanese national anthem ... literally. And if the mood takes you, you can even grab one of the dressing-up costumes and transform yourself into a giant bee. ⓐ B1F, 2-15, 12 Shinbashi, Minato-ku ⓣ 03 3591-2347 ⓛ 17.30–24.00 Mon–Sat Ⓜ Metro: Shinbashi

Lion Beer Hall Owned by the Sapporo Lion brewery, this beer hall will make you feel like you are out for a night in Munich due to its faux German interiors. Friday night karaoke always descends into singing chaos. 7-9-20 Ginza, Chuo-ku 03 3571 2590 www.ginzalion.jp 11.30–23.00 Mon–Sat, 11.30–22.30 Sun Metro: Ginza

Cinemas & theatres

Kabuki-za This theatre is probably the best in Tokyo for watching traditional *Kabuki* theatre. Performances can last for up to five hours, so the option of purchasing a ticket for a single act is great for those who just want to watch a little bit of this highly stylised theatrical form. 4-12-15 Ginza, Chuo-ku 03 3541 3131

The Kabuki-za theatre

ⓦ www.shochiku.co.jp ⓛ Box office: 10.00–18.00 ⓝ Metro: Higashi-Ginza

National Film Centre The purpose of this centre is to preserve and promote the study of cinema as an art form. Mini-festivals using films from the 19,000-strong collection are a constant feature, with themes revolving around e.g. German films of the 1930s through to Eastern European documentaries. With two cinemas onsite, there is always something screening. English-language options are common. ⓐ 3-7-6 Kyobashi, Chuo-ku ⓣ 03 3561 0823 ⓦ www.momat.co.jp ⓛ 11.00–18.00 Tues–Fri ⓝ Metro: Kyobashi

Tokyo Takarazuka Gekijo Takarazuka is a wildly popular Japanese entertainment form that takes females performers and transforms them into gender-bending stars. Productions are colourful, kitsch and extremely camp. The mainly female audience pines away at the androgynous 'males', yet there are no homosexual overtones whatsoever. You basically have to see it to believe it. Performances are in Japanese only.
ⓐ 1-1-3 Yurakucho, Chiyoda-ku ⓣ 03 5251 2001
ⓦ http://kakegi.hankyu.co.jp ⓛ Box office: 10.00–18.00 Mon & Tue, Thur–Sun ⓝ Metro: Yurakucho

North & east Tokyo: Akihabara, Asakusa & Ueno

Three communities, three atmospheres. For tradition and religious significance, Asakusa is the place to be. The entire district revolves around the activities of the Sensō-ji shrine, with action heating up in May when the Sanja Festival arrives. The normally conservative residents unshackle their inhibitions during this time and honour the goddess Kannon in a parade of drink, food and displays of strength.

Ueno, also a traditional community, is firmly blue collar. Here is where the merchants and traders of the Meiji period set up home. The working-class reputation remains, despite the fact that the area houses the largest concentration of world-class museums in the city. Go to Ueno Koen to explore the wealth of possibilities.

For a dose of modern culture, Akihabara is the place to go. Home to what could possible be the largest number of electronics shops in the world, it's a busy district packed with computers, MP3 players and neon.

SIGHTS & ATTRACTIONS

Hanayashiki

This amusement park is Tokyo's version of Coney Island – a bit on the old side, but loved by locals nonetheless. There are only about 20 rides, including one of Japan's oldest roller-coasters. A good place to bring the kids when they need a distraction from all the history.

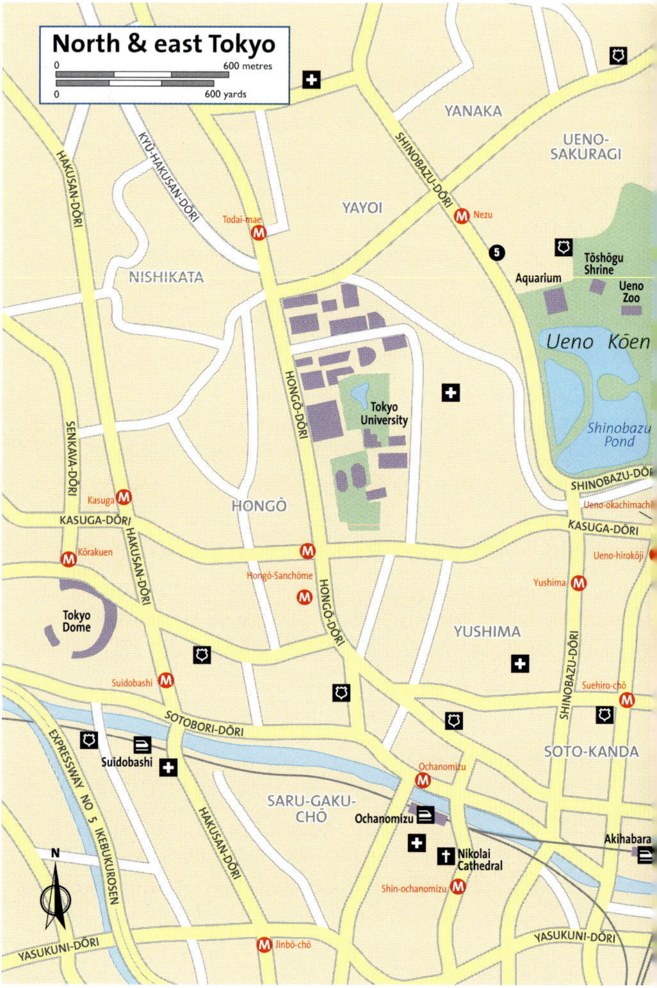

North & east Tokyo
0
600 metres
0
600 yards
YANAKA
UENO-SAKURAGI
SHINOBAZU-DŌRI
KYŪ-HAKUSAN-DŌRI
HAKUSAN-DŌRI
YAYOI
Todai-mae
Nezu
Tōshōgu Shrine
Aquarium
Ueno Zoo
NISHIKATA
Ueno Kōen
HONGŌ-DŌRI
Tokyo University
Shinobazu Pond
SENKAVA-DŌRI
SHINOBAZU-DŌRI
Kasuga
HONGŌ
Ueno-okachimachi
KASUGA-DŌRI
HAKUSAN-DŌRI
KASUGA-DŌRI
Kōrakuen
Hongō-Sanchōme
HONGŌ-DŌRI
Ueno-hirokōji
Yushima
Tokyo Dome
YUSHIMA
SHINOBAZU-DŌRI
Suidobashi
Suehiro-chō
SOTOBORI-DŌRI
EXPRESSWAY NO 5 IKEBUKUROSEN
Suidobashi
SOTO-KANDA
Ochanomizu
SARU-GAKU-CHŌ
HAKUSAN-DŌRI
Ochanomizu
Akihabara
N
Nikolai Cathedral
Shin-ochanomizu
YASUKUNI-DŌRI
Jinbō-chō
YASUKUNI-DŌRI

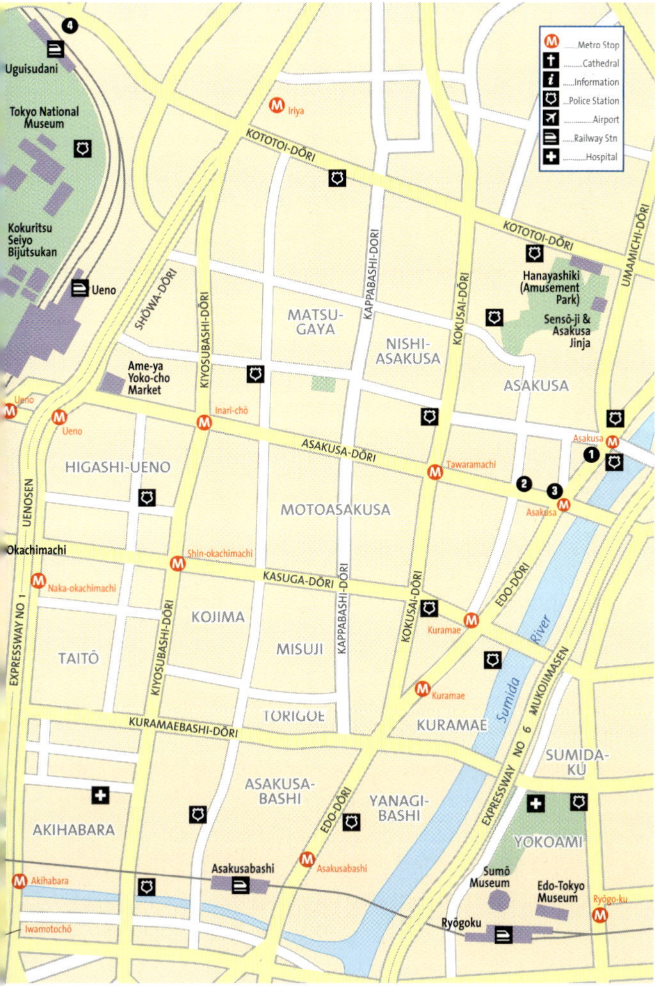
Metro Stop
Cathedral
Information
Police Station
Airport
Railway Stn
Hospital
Uguisudani
Tokyo National Museum
Kokuritsu Seiyo Bijutsukan
Ueno
Iriya
KOTOTOI-DŌRI
KOTOTOI-DŌRI
KAPPABASHI-DŌRI
KOKUSAI-DŌRI
UMAMICHI-DŌRI
Hanayashiki (Amusement Park)
Sensō-ji & Asakusa Jinja
MATSU-GAYA
NISHI-ASAKUSA
SHŌWA-DŌRI
KIYOSUBASHI-DŌRI
Ame-ya Yoko-cho Market
ASAKUSA
Ueno
Ueno
Inari-chō
ASAKUSA-DŌRI
Asakusa
Tawaramachi
HIGASHI-UENO
MOTOASAKUSA
Asakusa
UENOSEN
Okachimachi
Shin-okachimachi
KASUGA-DŌRI
Naka-okachimachi
KAPPABASHI-DŌRI
KOKUSAI-DŌRI
EDO-DŌRI
KOJIMA
Kuramae
River
EXPRESSWAY NO 1
MISUJI
TAITŌ
KIYOSUBASHI-DŌRI
MUKOJIMASEN
Kuramae
Sumida
TORIGOE
KURAMAEBASHI-DŌRI
KURAMAE
EXPRESSWAY NO 6
SUMIDA-KU
ASAKUSA-BASHI
YANAGI-BASHI
EDO-DŌRI
AKIHABARA
YOKOAMI
Asakusabashi
Asakusabashi
Sumō Museum
Edo-Tokyo Museum
Akihabara
Ryōgoku-ku
Ryōgoku
Iwamotochō

ⓐ 2-28-1 Asakusa, Taito-ku ⓣ 03 3842 8780
ⓦ www.hanayashiki.net Ⓜ Metro: Asakusa. Admission charge.

Sensō-ji (Asakusa Kannon Temple) & Asakusa Jinja
This temple complex is what the entire district of Asakusa revolves around. It acts as both a location of religious significance and the unofficial heart of the local community. Dedicated to the goddess Kannon, it is one of the only complexes in Japan that is important to both followers of Shinto and Buddhism. Highlights onsite include a five-storey pagoda and an incense burner reputed to give off smoke with curative powers. The best time to visit is during the Sanja Festival in May, when offerings are paraded through the streets of Asakusa before ending at the shrine.
ⓐ 2-3-1 Asakusa, Taito-ku ⓣ 03 3844 1575 ⓒ 06.00–17.00
Ⓜ Metro: Asakusa

Tōshōgu Shrine
Built to honour the first Tokogawa shogun, this shrine is considered a national treasure due to its resilience. The calamities of the 1868 revolt, 1923 earthquake and World War II firebombs destroyed most of the city, yet the shrine remained unaffected – making it one of the few examples of early Edo architecture in the capital. What makes this shrine so inspiring are the beautiful lanterns – more than 200 in total – that line the walkway from the entrance gate to the shrine itself. One of them, located just before the entry arch on the left, is one of the world's largest measuring almost 6 m (20 ft) in height. The two highlights of any tour are the first room inside the shrine

(known as the Hall of Worship) and the Chinese Gate. The Hall of Worship is renowned for its excellent examples of calligraphy and painting, while the Chinese Gate is admired for it carving and sculpture work.

ⓐ 9-88 Ueno Koen, Taito-ku ⓣ 03 3822 3455 ⓛ 09.00–18.00 ⓜ Metro: Ueno. Admission charge.

Ueno Koen

Tokyo's first public park is this strip of green space that stands on the site of a battle between supporters of the Tokugawa shogunate and Meiji government in the mid-19th century. Opened in 1873, it is no longer the largest public park in the city, although it remains one of the most loved. Inside the park is a wealth of diversions – including museums, shrines and a zoo. During cherry blossom season, the park can be swamped with admirers – all entranced by the vision of the delicate blooms.

ⓐ Ueno Koen, Taito-ku ⓛ 24 hrs ⓜ Metro: Ueno

CULTURE

Edo-Tokyo Museum

The history of the city is chronicled in this museum which takes a look at the development of Tokyo right back to its early days when it was a tiny fishing village called Edo. Developments are told using large-scale reconstructions and mock-ups. To get the most from a visit, join one of the regular English-language tours. While the museum isn't technically in any of the three districts covered in this section, it is reachable by taking a 5-minute metro jaunt from Akihabara.

A performer in Ueno Koen

ⓐ 1-4-1 Yokoami, Sumida-ku ⓣ 03 3626 9974 ⓦ www.edo-tokyo-museum.or.jp ⓒ 09.30–17.30 Tue & Wed, Sat & Sun, 09.30–20.00 Thur & Fri ⓝ Metro: Ryogoku. Admission charge.

Kokuritsu Seiyo Bijutsukan (National Museum of Western Art)
Industrialist Matsukata Kojiro compiled this collection during the first half of the 20th century but couldn't transport it to his home nation until after World War II. Kojiro bequeathed his holdings to the nation, resulting in the construction of this Le Corbusier-designed building which opened in 1959. The strongest works come from the French Impressionist period (including paintings by Renoir, Van Gogh and Monet), although additions have brought in more contemporary work from both Europe and the USA.
ⓐ 7-7 Ueno Koen ⓣ 03 3828 5131 ⓦ www.nmwa.go.jp
ⓒ 09.30–17.00 Tues–Thur, Sat & Sun, 09.30–20.00 Fri
ⓝ Metro: Ginza/Hibiya. Admission charge.

Tokyo National Museum
If you only have time to visit one museum, make it this one. Just as the Louvre or Hermitage are considered the world's greatest repositories of Western Art, so is this massive space to Eastern treasures. Linger over calligraphy, ceramics, paintings, sculptures, textiles, weaponry, masks and costumes that date back to 5000 BC. Three buildings make up the complex. To truly do it justice, you would need at least a day.
ⓐ 13-9 Ueno Koen, Taito-ku ⓣ 03 3822 1111 ⓦ www.tnm.go.jp
ⓒ 09.30–17.00 Tues–Sun ⓝ Metro: Ueno. Admission charge.

A Le Corbusier building houses the National Museum of Western Art

RETAIL THERAPY

Shopping streets & markets

Akihabara If it bleeps, computes, is programmable or possesses a heap of circuits and microchips, then chances are you will find it on the streets of Akihabara. Electronics are the raison d'être of this district with cutting-edge technology literally dripping out of every shop. Prices aren't cheap. In fact, if you're looking for a bargain, you'd be better off making a purchase in New York. That, combined with the fact that everything only comes with Japanese instructions (and in many cases Japanese buttons) means you should be wary before shelling out your yen. What makes this neighbourhood such a Mecca for geeks and nerds is that this is where you'll find the latest and greatest versions of every techno-trinket on the market, often years before they hit the streets of the Western world. When you emerge from the station, the volume of neon can be overwhelming – as can the marketing flyers you'll be handed. Dotted among the superstores are manga comic shops and fast food outlets – all the things a good geek needs to survive.

Ame-ya Yoko-cho Market The end of World War II saw much hardship for the Japanese, with many basic necessities almost impossible to come by. The area around Ueno station quickly became notorious as a massive black market – a reputation it still maintains. Today, it is the source for knock-offs and designer fakes. Ask around to find the best merchants, as they will usually keep their best wares hidden away. During the two weeks around Christmas and New Year, the stalls can be crammed with more than half-million people in search of a bargain. ⓐ Ueno 4-chome, Taito-ku ◷ 10.00–19.00 Ⓜ Metro: Ueno

TAKING A BREAK

ef £ ❶ Asakusa has a reputation for being a little on the conservative side. This coffee shop attempts to dispel the neighbourhood's fuddy-duddy image by thrusting a little cool into the community. The front of the establishment is a small art gallery featuring works by locals and students. Go to the back for a cup of coffee and a cake in the tatami-mat café. A great place to revive after a day of temple hopping. ⓐ 2-19-18 Kaminarimon, Taito-ku ⓣ 03 3841 0114 ⓦ www.gallery-ef.com ◷ 11.00–24.00 Mon, Wed, Thur & Sat, 11.00–02.00 Fri, 11.00–22.00 Sun Ⓜ Metro: Asakusa

AFTER DARK

Restaurants

Aoi-Marushin £ ❷ This large establishment serves tempura dishes that are light, yet crispy, It's a good option for fussy kids, as you can get away with telling them it's like eating fish and chips. ⓐ 1-4-4 Asakusa, Taito-ku ⓣ 03 3841 0110 ◷ 10.00–21.00 Ⓜ Metro: Asakusa

Tatsumiya ££ ❸ As befits such a traditional community, this restaurant serves meals in the *kaiseki* style – seven courses, each with a different traditional requirement. During the meal, you

Confectionery comes artistically packaged in Asakusa

will need to have something vinegared, grilled, raw and boiled. It's a long process, so check what time you need to arrive to enjoy the full event. ⓐ 1-33-5 Asakusa, Taito-ku ⓣ 03 3842 7373 ◷ 11.00–22.00 Tues–Sun Ⓜ Metro: Asakusa

Sasa-no-yuki £££–£££ ❹ For over three centuries, this dining spot has been serving up vegetarian dishes using tofu as a base. The menu draws its inspiration from the principles of Buddhist vegetarian cuisine. ⓐ 2-15-10 Negishi, Taito-ku ⓣ 03 3873 1145 ◷ 11.00–20.00 Tues–Sun Ⓜ Metro: Uguisudani

Hantei £££ ❺ Course after course of skewered meat, veggies and fish grilled to perfection. Traditional barbecue joints tend to be rustic, but this one is delightfully atmospheric. Staff will continue serving dishes in series of six courses. After the sixth course, you can either have another six or ask them to stop. Unless you say something, the food will just keep coming. ⓐ 2-12-15 Nezu, Bunkyo-ku ⓣ 03 3828 1440 ◷ 12.00–14.30, 17.00–22.00 Tues–Sat, 16.00–21.30 Sun Ⓜ Metro: Nezu

Bars, clubs & discos

Flamme d'Or It's easy to find the location of this drinking spot owned by the Asahi brewery – just look for the bizarre Philippe Starck-designed gold sculpture at the top of the building in which it is located. The beer hall is a bit like a cross between an airport lounge and a pub. It may lack ambience, but it certainly has plenty on tap to choose from. ⓐ Asahi Super Dry Hall 1F-2F, 1-23-36 Azumabashi, Sumida-ku ⓣ 03 5608 5381 ◷ 11.30–23.00 June–Aug, 11.30–22.00 Sept–May Ⓜ Metro: Asakusa

Kamiya Bar Picture the kind of place your electrician or builder might go to and chances are you'd come up with an image of the Kamiya. Blue-collar locals call this dark and atmospheric place home – and have done so ever since the establishment was founded in the late 19th century. Look closely and you may even spot an overflowing ashtray that dates back to the period. The place to go if you want to meet true characters and enjoy a drink without all the pretensions. ⓐ 1-1-1 Asakusa, Taito-ku ⓣ 03 3841 5400 ⓦ www.kamiya-bar.com ⓛ 11.30–22.00 Mon, Wed–Sun ⓝ Metro: Asakusa

CINEMA & THEATRE

Suzumoto Storytelling is the oldest form of theatrical performance in the world and this theatre is one of the oldest in Tokyo performing the ancient craft. Each performance employs the same format: a lone comedian will take to the centre of the stage, sit in a kimono on a purple cushion and tell a story. Only a few props are used, but facial expressions and vocal intonations do the rest in terms of character definition. There is no English translation – and the dialects make it hard for even locals to understand – but well worth checking out. ⓐ 2-7-12 Ueno Koen, Taito-ku ⓣ 03 3834 5906 ⓛ 12.20–16.30, 17.20–21.10 ⓝ Metro: Ueno Hiroko-ji

South & west Tokyo: Aoyama, Harajuku, Roppongi, Shibuya & Shinjuku

The neighbourhoods of south and west Tokyo are less famous for their sights than they are for their nightclubs, fashions, boutiques and glittering lights. Basically, you come here to stop feeding your mind and fill up on self-indulgence. Each of the districts lies on or near the loop line that travels clockwise from Tokyo station, with Roppongi the first in the series.

For years, Roppongi was the area of choice for Western tourists and expats. While it still holds that reputation, the recent development of the ultra-hip Roppongi Hills complex is slowly beginning to add a touch of chic.

Next lies Shibuya with its trashy teen culture and chain-street shopping. If you want to watch Tokyo go by like Scarlett Johansson did in the film *Lost in Translation*, follow in her steps by sipping a coffee at the Starbucks overlooking Shibuya crossing.

Next up are Harajuku and Aoyama – two distinctly different neighbourhoods catering to two totally different shoppers. Aoyama boasts all the big name designer shops, including one of the largest branches of Prada in the world. Harajuku, meanwhile, is home to street fashion and cutting-edge trends.

Finally, there is Shinjuku, the nightclub capital of the city. Head here for a bit of a boogie to hard techno beats, or explore the gay ghetto with its more than 300 bars.

SIGHTS & ATTRACTIONS

Meiji Shrine & Inner Garden

Destroyed by the bombs of World War II, this shrine was rebuilt in 1958 and is now one of the most visited in the city. It honours the life of Emperor Meiji, thought by many to be the father of contemporary Japan. While it isn't as visually stirring as other temple complexes due to its sparse Shinto design, it hosts a number of festivals which contribute to its popularity.
ⓐ 1-1 Yoyogi-Kamizomocho, Shibuya-ku ⓣ 03 3379 5511
ⓦ www.meijijingu.or.jp ⓛ Sunrise–sunset ⓜ Metro: Harajuku. Admission charge for Meiji Shrine Garden and Treasure House only.

Many popular festivals are held in the Meiji Shrine

Nakano
Nakano
NAKANO-KU
Higashi-Nakano
Higashi Nakano
ŌKUBO-DŌRI
Ōkubo
Shin-ōkubo
MEIJI-DŌRI
ŌKUBO-DŌRI
Wakamatsu-kawada
OTAKIBASHI-DŌRI
Higashi-shinjuku
SHOKUAN-DŌRI
Shin-nakano
Nakano-Sakaue
ŌME-KAIDŌ
Nishi-shinjuku
Seibu-shinjuku
CHŪŌ
SHINJUKU-KU
KŌEN-DŌRI
Tochōmae
HIGASHI-DŌRI
Shinjuku-sanchōme
YASUKUNI-DŌRI
Akebonobashi
Nakano-shinbashi
Nakano-fujimi-chō
Nishi-shinjuku-gochōme
Shinjuku
Shinjuku
Shinjukugyoenmae
SHINJUKU-DŌRI
Yotsuyasanchōme
Tokyo Metropolitan Government Building No. 1
KŌSHŪ-KAIDŌ
HŌNAN-DŌRI
Shinjuku Gyoen Garden
Fire Museum
SUGINAMI-KU
PATIO-DŌRI
Minami-shinjuku
Yoyogi
Sendagaya
NAKANO-DŌRI
New National Theatre Tokyo
Shinanomachi
EXPRESSWAY NO 4 SHINJUKUSEN
Sangūbashi
National Noh Theatre
GAIEN-NISHI-DŌRI
National Stadium
Hatagaya
HATSUDAI
MEIJI-DŌRI
Sasazuka
Sasazuka
YAMATE-DŌRI
Meiji Shrine & Inner Garden
AOYAMA
HARAJUKU
Yoyogi Park
Yoyogi-Uehara
Yoyogi-Uehara
Yoyogihachiman
Harajuku
Tokyo Hands Department Store
SHIBUYA-KU
Gaienmae
Yoyogikōenmae
Meijijingūmae
INOKASHIRA-DŌRI
OMOTESANDO AVE
Tōkai University
NHK Broadcasting Center
Omotesandō
Tobacco & Salt Museum
MEIJI-DŌRI
Shimo-kitazawa
Ikenoue
Tokyo University
AOYAMA-DŌRI
N
Shibuya
Shibuya
Komaba-tōdaimae
SETAGAYA-KU
Shinsen
Shibuya
MEIJI-DŌRI
EXPRESSWAY NO 3 SHIBUYASEN
KOMAZAWA-DŌRI
Ikejiri-ōhashi
Setagaya Public Theatre
Sangenjaya
Sangenjaya
MEGURO-KU
YAMATE-DŌRI
Daikanyama
Ebisu
Ebisu
1
2
3
4
6
7
8
9

South & west Tokyo
0
1000 metres
0
1000 yards
Metro Stop
Cathedral
Information
Police Station
Airport
Railway Stn
Hospital
Kōrakuen
Hongō-San chōme
Tokyo Dome
Suidobashi
Kagurazaka
Ushigome kagurazaka
Iidabashi
WASEDA-DŌRI
SOTOBORI-DŌRI
HONGŌ-DŌRI
SHINOBAZU-DŌRI
EXPRESSWAY NO 5 IKEBUKUROSEN
ŌKUBO-DŌRI
Ushigome Yanagi-chō
YARAICHŌ
IIDABASHI
MEJIRO-DŌRI
Ochanomizu
Shin-ochanomizu
Kanda River
Kudanshita
Jinbō-chō
Ogawamachi
Awaji-chō
Iwamotochō
KANDA
KANDAHEISEI-DŌRI
Kanda
Ichigaya Hachiman-chō
YASUKUNI-DŌRI
Ichigaya
Kakagu Gijutsukan
INNER LOOP EXP
EXPRESSWAY NO 1 UENOSEN
Kodenma-chō
National Museum of Modern Art
KUDAN-MINAMI
UCHIBORI-DŌRI
CHŪŌ-DŌRI
KŌSOKUTOSHINKANJŌSEN
Mitsukoshimae
Yotsuya
Hanzōmon
Kōjimachi
Fukiage Garden
Ōtemachi
SHINJUKU-DŌRI
HIBIYA-DŌRI
WAKABA
Imperial Palace
Imperial Agency
Tokyo
Nihonbashi
National Theatre
Supreme Court
Nijubashimae
MARUNOUCHI
YAESU-DŌRI
Kayaba-chō
State Guesthouse
Shinkansen
Kyōbashi
Takara-chō
Hatchōbori
MOTO-AKASAKA
Nagata-chō
Sakuradamon
Akasakamitsuke
Tokyo High Court
Yūraku-chō
Hibiya Park
Hibiya
Kokkaigijidōmae
Ginza-itchōme
Aoyamaitchōme
Akasaka
Kasumigaseki
Tameike-sannō
Ginza
AKASAKA
SAKURADA-DŌRI
ATAGO-DŌRI
HIBIYA-DŌRI
Shintomi-chō
Ōkura Shūkokan Museum
Toranomon
Uchisaiwai-chō
Higashi-ginza
Kabukiza Theatre
Odaiba
GINZA
Tsukiji
Nogizaka
Shinbashi
Tsukijishijō
SHIN'ŌHASHI-DŌRI
CHŪŌ-KU
MINATO-KU
Sumida River
Roppongi-Itchōme
Kamiya-chō
Shiodome
HARUMI-DŌRI
EXPRESSWAY NO 3 SHIBUYASEN
ROPPONGI
Roppongi
Tokyo Tower
EXP NO 1 HANEDASEN
Tokyo Central Wholesale Market
TSUKIJI
Onarimon
Mori Art Museum & Tokyo City View
International Culture Hall
Zōjō-ji Temple
Hama-Rikyū Onshi Teien
Kachi-doki
Daimon
Akabanebashi
Azabujūban
EXPRESSWAY NO 2 MEGUROSEN
Shibakōen
Hamamatsuchō
MITA

Tokyo Metropolitan Government Building No. 1

The best view in Tokyo – and it's completely free! Zip your way up to the 45th floor. On clear days, you can even see the peak of Mount Fuji in the distance.

ⓐ 2-8-1 Nishi-Shinjuku, Shinjuku-ku ⓣ 03 5321 1111
ⓛ North Observatory: 09.30–23.00 Tues–Sun; South Observatory: 09.30–17.30 Mon, Wed–Sun ⓜ Metro: Tochomae

Tokyo Tower

The construction of Tokyo Tower was a statement to the rest of the world that Tokyo had arrived. It marked the end of post-war hardship and firmly thrust the city into a superleague of its own. Resembling the Eiffel Tower in Paris, it is now dwarfed by nearby skyscrapers and is no longer worth going up due to the lack of views. From other buildings, though, it looks stunning and is a true symbol of the city.

ⓐ 4-2-8 Shiba-Koen, Minato-ku ⓣ 03 3433 5111
ⓦ www.tokyotower.co.jp ⓛ 09.00–22.00 ⓜ Metro: Kamiyacho. Admission charge.

Zōjō-ji Temple

The three sections of this temple complex and mausoleum are dedicated to the depiction of the three stages all humans require to reach Nirvana – a central teaching of the Buddhist Jodo sect for whom this centre of worship was created. Keep a look out for the heartbreaking statues of Jizu, the keeper of the souls of miscarried and stillborn babies, for whom thousands of women leave offerings every day in honour of their own departed children.

ⓐ 4-7-35 Shiba-Koen, Minato-ku ⓣ 03 3432 1431 ⓦ zojoji.or.jp
ⓛ 06.00–17.30 ⓜ Metro: Shiba-Koen

CULTURE

Fire Museum

While the displays chronicling the fire-fighting service of the city are intriguing, it's the videos and outlines of the devastation fire caused following the Great Kanto Earthquake of 1923 and fire-bombing during World War II that are the true draws. A great addition to your knowledge of the social history of the capital.
ⓐ 3-10 Yotsuya, Shinjuku-ku ⓣ 03 3353 9119 ⓛ 09.30–17.00 Tues–Sun ⓜ Metro: Yotsuya-Sanchome

Tokyo Tower was first opened in 1958

ODAIBA

Odaiba is Tokyo's newest district – and a futuristic one at that. The entire region is made from land reclaimed from Tokyo Bay. The most inspirational building is the Fuji TV headquarters, topped by a huge metal sphere, which offers amazing views.

The Odeo Onsen Monogatari complex looks like an Edo-period village complete with food stalls and games, and can be used as an overnight rest-stop. But Mega Web is the main draw on Odaiba. The Ferris wheel is loved by courting couples, while petrol heads love the automotive museum and Toyota showroom.

There are several maritime-inspired museums, including the Museum of Maritime Science and Waterworks Science Museum. Displays at the two museums include a ride down a virtual river.

Finally, there's the National Museum of Emerging Science which takes a fascinating look at the potential innovations of tomorrow. Even if you hate science, this museum will inspire you.

Fuji Television Nippon Broadcasting Building ⓐ 2-4-8 Daiba, Minato-ku ⓣ 03 5500 8888 ◷ 10.00–20.00 Tues–Sun Ⓜ Metro: Daiba. Admission charge.
Mega Web ⓐ 1 Aomi, Koto-ku ⓣ 03 3599 0808 ⓦ www.megaweb.gr.jp ◷ 11.00–23.00 Ⓜ Metro: Aomi
Museum of Maritime Science ⓐ 3-1 Higashi-Yashio, Shinagawa-ku ⓣ 03 5500 1111 ◷ 10.00–17.00 Mon–Fri, 10.00–18.00 Sat & Sun Ⓜ Metro: Funeno-Kagakukan. Admission charge.

National Museum of Emerging Science and Innovation ⓐ 2-41 Aomi, Koto-ku ⓣ 03 3570 9151 10.00–19.00 Mon, Wed–Sat, 10.00–17.00 Sun Metro: Telecom Center. Admission charge.

Odeo Onsen Monogatari ⓐ 2-57 Omi, Koto-ku ⓣ 03 5500 1126 11.00–09.00 Metro: Telecom Center. Admission charge.

Tokyo Metropolitan Waterworks Science Museum ⓐ 2-4-1 Ariake, Koto-ku ⓣ 03 3528 2366 09.30–17.00 Tues–Sun Metro: Kokusai Tenjijo-Seimon

The Ferris wheel in Odaiba

Mori Art Museum & Tokyo City View

Contemporary art in a spectacular setting. Spend half your time admiring the always-strong temporary exhibits and the other half admiring the views from the 52nd floor. The fact that it is located within the socially hip Roppongi Hills development adds to the crowds.

ⓐ Mori Tower 52-53F, 6-10-1 Roppongi, Minato-ku ⓣ 03 6406 6100 ⓛ 10.00–22.00 Mon, Wed & Thur, 10.00–17.00 Tue, 10.00–24.00 Fri & Sat ⓜ Metro: Roppongi. Admission charge.

Tobacco & Salt Museum

The two commodities of salt and tobacco were once so treasured that the importation of them was controlled by the state. This museum looks at the social and economic impact tobacco and salt have had on the nation with everything from marketing techniques to accoutrements on display. The cigarette advertisements are particularly eye-opening.

ⓐ 1-16-8 Jinnan, Shibuya-ku ⓣ 03 3476 2041 ⓛ 10.00–18.00 Tues–Sun ⓜ Metro: Shibuya. Admission charge.

RETAIL THERAPY

Shopping streets & markets

The neighbourhoods of south and west Tokyo are all about shopping, so it's hard to focus on a single region. For designer goods, go straight to Omotesando station and explore the works of both Japanese and Western couturiers. Harajuku is the port of call for those wanting to explore the often wild and unwearable world of street fashion. Be warned, trends come and go in a heartbeat, so you may find the spectacular accessory you pick up today is gone tomorrow. Shibuya is full of typical teenagers. Go here for CDs to add to the collection and high-street chains. Meanwhile, Shinjuku is department store and shopping centre heaven. The Tokyo Hands department store at Harajuku station is a particular standout due to its wealth of kitsch.

TAKING A BREAK

Heiroku-zushi ££ ❶ Yo! Sushi pales in comparison to this conveyor-belt establishment which offers fresh, fast delicacies prepared by sushi chefs who know their stuff. Take as many plates as you want, then your server will add up the cost based on the number of dishes and specialties you selected. ⓐ 5-8-5 Jingumae, Shibuya-ku ⓣ 03 3498 3968 ⓛ 11.00–21.00 ⓜ Metro: Omotesando

AFTER DARK

Restaurants

Kyushu Jangara Ramen £ ❷ This ramen noodle outlet is perfect for those wanting a small dollop of food or a massive bowl – depending on how hungry you are. Choose your own broth, ingredients and amount of noodles. ⓐ Shanzeru Harajuku Ni-go-kan 1F-2F, 1-13-21 Jingumae, Shibuya-ku ⓣ 03 3404 5572 ⓛ 11.00–02.00 Mon–Thur, Sun, 11.00–15.30 Fri & Sat ⓜ Metro: Meijijingumae

Ume no Hana £ ❸ You'll never believe how many ways tofu can be prepared until you make a stop at this eatery which

serves it up in every way imaginable. All appetizers, main courses and desserts feature tofu. And it's cheap too!
ⓐ 2-14-6 Kita-Aoyama, Bell Commons 3F, Minato-ku
ⓣ 03 3475 8077 ⓛ 11.00–15.00, 17.00–21.00 ⓜ Metro: Gaienmae

Yukun-tei £ ❹ Small, yet cheery dining spot specialising in the dishes of the island of Kyushu. The sake is exceptionally good.
ⓐ 3-26 Arakicho, Shinjuku-ku ⓣ 03 3356 3351 ⓛ 11.30–14.00, 17.00–22.30 Mon–Sat ⓜ Metro: Yotsuya-Sanchome

Ganchan ££ ❺ The Japanese dish of yakitori is a bit like their version of the traditional greasy spoon. You'll know if you've walked into a good one if the servers are brusque, the chefs are loud and the place is packed. Yakitori is essentially barbecued chicken and vegetables grilled to perfection.
ⓐ 6-8-23 Roppongi, Minato-ku ⓣ 03 3478 0092 ⓛ 05.30–01.30 Mon–Sat, 05.30–24.00 Sun ⓜ Metro: Roppongi

Hannibal £££ ❻ The flavours of North Africa come alive at this delightful Tunisian restaurant. Probably the best place in the city to get a meal inspired by the tastes and spices of the Arab world. ⓐ Urban Bldg B1F, 1-11-1 Hyakunincho, Shinjuku-ku
ⓣ 03 5389 7313 ⓦ www.hannibal.cc ⓛ 17.30–24.30 Mon–Sat
ⓜ Metro: Shin-Okubo

Le Papillon de Paris £££ ❼ If you ever wanted to know what it's like to parade down a fashion catwalk, then a stroll through this restaurant, with interiors designed by Japanese couturier Hanae Mori, should give you an idea. As there are only a few seats in the place, reservations are a must – and should be planned if you are a fan of fine French food. ⓐ Hanae Mori Bldg, 5th Fl, 3-6-1 Kita-Aoyama, Minato-ku ⓣ 03 3407 7461 ⓛ 11.30–15.30, 17.30–23.00 Mon–Sat, 11.30–15.30 Sun ⓜ Metro: Omotesando

New York Grill £££ ❽ When locals want to do a power lunch, they do it over big, fat American steaks – and this dining spot in the Park Hyatt Hotel is just the place. If you're in town for business and want to close the deal, then make a reservation here. ⓐ Park Hyatt Hotel, 52nd Fl, 3-7-1-2 Nishi-Shinjuku, Shinjuku-ku ⓣ 03 5323 3458 ⓦ www.parkhyatttokyo.com ⓛ 11.30–02.30, 05.30–22.00 ⓜ Metro: Shinjuku

Nobu Tokyo £££ ❾ Loved by celebrities, this branch of the famous global Nobu sushi chain serves the Latin-inspired sushi dishes for which the restaurant is renowned. While Nobu is originally from Tokyo, he made his name abroad and is therefore not as celebrated in his hometown as he is in the Western world. ⓐ 6-10-17 Minami-Aoyama, Minato-ku ⓣ 03 5467 0022 ⓦ www.soho-s.co.jp ⓛ 11.30–15.30, 18.00–23.30 Mon–Fri, 18.00–23.30 Sat ⓜ Metro: Omotesando

Spago £££ ❿ Celebrity chef Wolfgang Puck opened this branch of his famous restaurant specialising in Californian cuisine. Dishes are characteristic of the flavours of the American West coast with a strong focus on oven-baked pizzas and light pastas. ⓐ 5-7-8 Roppongi, Minato-ku ⓣ 03 3423 4025 ⓛ 11.30–14.00, 18.00–22.00 Mon–Fri, 11.30–14.00, 18.00–21.30 Sat & Sun ⓜ Metro: Roppongi

Bars, clubs & discos

Advocates Bar Due to its location in the middle on a major corner in the centre of Shinjuku's gay ghetto, Advocates is one of the most popular meeting spots for Western gay men and their local admirers. The basement dance floor is always popular – sometimes to the point of claustrophobia. ⓐ 7th Tenka Bldg B1F, 2-18-1 Shinjuku, Shinjuku-ku ⓣ 03 3358 8638 ⓛ 20.00–04.00 ⓝ Metro: Shinjuku-Sanchome

Arty-Farty Shinjuku's most popular gay nightclub, and welcoming to Westerners. Boasts a Tex-Mex interior. ⓐ Dai 33 Kyutei Bldg 2F, 2-11-6 Shinjuku, Shinjuku-ku ⓣ 03 3356 5388 ⓦ www.arty-farty.net ⓛ 19.00–24.00 Mon, 19.00–05.00 Tues–Fri, 17.00–05.00 Sat & Sun ⓝ Metro: Shinjuku-Sanchome

Big Echo Tokyo's largest karaoke chain has literally dozens of branches scattered throughout the city. This location, in the heart of Roppongi, is one of the busiest. ⓐ 7-14-12 Roppongi, Minato-ku ⓣ 03 5770 7700 ⓛ 18.00–05.00 ⓝ Metro: Hibiya

Blue Note Tokyo Big jazz names perform here on a regular basis, while Japanese talent sets the tone on Sunday evenings. Previous concerts have seen the Count Basie Orchestra and Herbie Hancock grace the stage. ⓐ 6-3-16 Minami-Aoyama, Minato-ku ⓣ 03 5485 0088 ⓦ www.bluenote.co.jp ⓛ 19.00 & 21.30 Mon–Sat, 18.30 & 21.00 Sun ⓝ Metro: Omotesando

New York Bar The setting for the famous scenes from the film *Lost in Translation*. The views are spectacular from this stylish drinking den on the 52nd floor. Frequent jazz performers merely add to the splendour. ⓐ Park Hyatt Hotel, 52nd Floor, 3-7-1-2 Nishi-Shinjuku, Shinjuku-ku ⓣ 03 5322 1234 ◷ 17.00–24.00 Mon–Wed & Sun, 17.00–01.00 Thur–Sat ⓝ Metro: Tocho-mae

Secobar Often touted as one of the friendliest clubs in Tokyo, this drinking den located under a set of very noisy railway tracks is a café by day and a hip dance spot at sundown. Music selections change every night from salsa to deep house. ⓐ 3-23-1 Shibuya, Shibuya-ku ⓣ 03 5778 4571 ⓦ www.secobar.jp ◷ 11.00–05.00 ⓝ Metro: Shibuya

Smash Hits With more English-language songs available than any other karaoke bar in Tokyo, this singing spot is a favourite with expats and foreign visitors. ⓐ 5-2-26 Hiro-o, Shibuya-ku ⓣ 03 3444 0432 ⓦ www.smashhits.jp ◷ 19.00–03.00 Mon–Sat ⓝ Metro: Hibiya

Space Lab Yellow Progressive house and drum 'n' bass played well into the wee hours. The multiple levels make it a good choice for those who want to both lounge and live it up. ⓐ 1-10-11 Nishi-Azabu, Minato-ku ⓣ 03 3479 0690 ⓦ www.club-yellow.com ◷ 22.00–late ⓝ Metro: Nogizaka

Womb International talent such as Richie Hawtin and Danny Howells make this club their home while in town. Minimalist techno is what you'll find most evenings. Expect beats to be hard and the liquor even harder. ⓐ 2-16 Maruyama-cho, Shibuya-ku ⓣ 03 5459 0039 ⓦ www.womb.co.jp ◷ 22.00–late ⓝ Metro: Shibuya

Cinemas & theatres

National Noh Theatre *Noh* is an ancient and highly ritualistic theatrical form dating back to the 14th century. The central performer wears a mask and there are always scenes of dance, war, lyrical beauty and demonic retribution. Let's just say, it isn't an evening of light entertainment. Performances are staged five times per year. ⓐ 4-18-1 Sendagaya, Shibuya-ku ⓣ 03 3230 3000 ⓦ www.ntj.jac.co.jp Box office: 10.00–18.00 Metro: Sandagaya

New National Theatre, Tokyo Three theatrical and concert spaces cater to the classical lovers of the city. Here is where you will see performances from the world-class Tokyo Symphony Orchestra and the Fujiwara Opera Company. ⓐ 1-1-1 Honmachi, Shibuya-ku ⓣ 03 5352 9999 ⓦ www.nntt.jac.go.jp Box office: 10.00–19.00 Metro: Hatsudai

Setagaya Public Theatre The best place to see Butoh, a form of Japanese dance that draws much from both Eastern and Western contemporary techniques. A Butoh dance is instantly recognisable because its performers have shaved heads, are covered in white body paint and move very slowly. ⓐ 4-1-1 Tashido, Setagaya-ku ⓣ 03 5432 1526 ⓦ www.setagaya-ac.or.jp Box office: 10.00–19.00 Metro: Sangenjaya

Bullet trains will take you to Yokohama in just 15 minutes

OUT OF TOWN trips

Fuji-san (Mount Fuji), Fuji Go-ko (Fuji Five Lakes) & Hakone

FUJI-SAN (MOUNT FUJI)

Probably Japan's most famous icon, Mount Fuji (3,776 m/ 12,389 ft) is actually a dormant volcano that last erupted in 1707. Almost 200,000 people try to climb Mount Fuji every year, tempted by its symmetrical beauty and religious significance. There are six trails to choose from, but only two are recommended for novices: the northern route leaving from Go-gome (Fifth Station), and the southern route departing from Shin-Go-gome (New Fifth Station). Both stations are accessible by bus. If you want to make it easier on yourself, use the shorter path of Go-gome and descend using the volcanic sand slide on the Shin-Go-gome side. Expect the climb to take a minimum of five hours.

! In order to complete the climb successfully, make sure you bring a backpack containing plenty of food and water. While huts along the route provide supplies, they are notoriously expensive. The backpack also comes in handy for using the volcanic sand slide, as you'll need something to sit on. Wear lots of layers to deal with changing temperatures and make sure you have sunscreen on, as the high altitude rays can bake.

! The official climbing period lasts from 1 July–26 August. Outside these dates, it is considered folly to attempt a summit by yourself. Not only is the weather unpredictable, but also there far fewer adventurers who could potentially assist you in the event of an accident.

Kawaguchiko Tourist Information ⓐ 3631-5 Funatsu, Kawaguchiko-Machi ⓣ 05 5572 6700 ⓛ 08.30–17.00

GETTING THERE

While it is possible to take the train to Mount Fuji from Tokyo, it does involve a lot of line changing and you'll eventually need to take a coach once you reach Kawaguchiko station. A better option is to take one of the six daily buses from Shinjuku station straight to Go-gome (Fifth Stage). Journey time is 2½ hours.

WHERE TO STAY

If you get tired during your climb, there are rest huts at stations along the way. These stations are only effective as places to pause, grab a hot drink and rest your feet. Renting one of the beds is not recommended. The sheets are rarely changed and the mattresses are far from comfortable. Dozing on the rocky trails in the rain would probably be more comfortable.

FUJI GO-KO (FUJI FIVE LAKES)

The Fuji Five Lakes region to the north of the mountain is a popular base for both climbers and those who just want to take in the views. A wealth of water activities such as kayaking and speedboating are a great tonic to those who have felt cooped up in the urban jungle of Tokyo.

The two most developed lakes of Yamanaka and Kawaguchi are popular with those in search of resort-style accommodation, while the other three lakes of Sai, Shoji and Motosu are more rustic in feel.

Tokyo region
0
15 km
0
10 miles
N
Kanto-sanchi
Chichibu
SAITAMA
Okutama
YAMANASHI
Yamanashi
Enzan
Nirasaki
Kōfu
Ōtsuki
Ichikawadaimon
Kawaguchi-ko
Kawaguchiko
Sai-ko
Shoji-ko
Motosu-ko
Fujiyoshida
Yamanaka-ko
Go-gome
Fuji-San
3776
Yamanokako
Shin-Go-gome
Minobu
Gotemba
Odawara
Owaku-dani
Togendai
Hakone
Ashino-ko
Fujinomiya
Fuji
Mishima
Yui
Numazu
Atami
SHIZUOKA
Shimizu
Ōhito
Shizuoka
Itō
Suruga-wan
City
Large Town
Small Town
POI
Motorway
Main Road
Minor Road
Airport
Railway

Kasukabe
Kawagoe
Ōmiya
Koshigaya
Abiko
Sayama
Urawa
Nagareyama
Iruma
Niza
Tokorozawa
Kawaguchi
TOKYO
Hōya
Funabashi
Musashino
Ichikawa
Koganei
Mitaka
TOKYO
Hachiōji
Shinjuku
Shiodome
Urayasu
Chiba
Komae
Sagamihara
Hameda
Tokyo-wan
Kawasaki
Ichihara
NAGAWA
tsugi
Yokohama
Kisarazu
Fujisawa
Kamakura
Hiratsuka
Yokosuka
CHIBA
Futtsu
Sagami-wan
Miura
China
Tateyama
Tokyo region
Japan
Sagami-nada

Kawaguchiko Tourist Information @ 3631-5 Funatsu, Kawaguchiko-Machi ⓣ 05 5572 6700 ⓛ 08.30–17.00

GETTING THERE

Take one of the hourly buses from Shinjuku station to Lake Kawaguchi. Departures are available at ten minutes past the hour from 07.10–20.10 daily.

Kawaguchi-ko

In terms of tourist attractions and hotels, Kawaguchi-ko is by far the most developed. This is the lake to come to if you want the famous shot of the mountain reflected into the water. Take the cable-car ride to the top of Tenjo-san (Mount Tenjo) for an inspiring view of the lake with Mount Fuji just beyond.

Motosu-ko

The journey to this lake is the longest, as it is the furthest to the west. As the water is so deep and clear, it is great for those looking for a reviving swim in near silence. Your bus journey from Kawaguchi-ko station will take about an hour.

Sai-ko

The third-largest lake combines rural splendour with a touch of development. Go to the western side to enjoy the best views of Mount Fuji. If you like exploring caves, there are two nearby which can be reached by following the signposted trail. Regular buses from Kawaguchi-ko station make the short journey to the lake.

Shoji-ko

This lake is the smallest of the lot and consequently the least developed. A big hit with trail walkers is the Shoji trail, which

FUN OF THE FAIR: FUJIKYU HIGHLAND

Popular with both expats and locals alike, this amusement park is on the hit-list of most coaster fanatics due to its possession of the fastest roller-coaster in the world. Step aboard and count to ten before being shot out into a pitch-black tunnel that will see you wishing you were back on solid ground.

ⓐ 5-6-1 Shin Nishi Hara, Fujiyoshida-shi ⓣ 05 5523-2111 🕒 09.00–17.00 Mon–Fri, 09.00–20.00 Sat & Sun. Admission charge.

Visit Fujikyu Highland for the ride of your life

leads to Mount Fuji through a beautiful forest known as Aoki-ga-hara (Sea of Trees). To get here, take the regular bus from Kawaguchi-ko station.

❶ It is advisable to use a (human) guide, as the lava field that flows under the area is magnetic and can cause your compass to give false readings!

Yamanaka-ko

The largest lake of the five is popular primarily due to its proximity to the easy Go-gome trail up Mount Fuji. Many climbers use the hotels and resorts here as a convenient base. Journey time from Kawaguchi-ko station is just over 30 minutes.

ACCOMMODATION

Inn Fujitomita £ Cheap and efficient, this property is really good value due to the onsite swimming pool, complimentary shuttle service from the train station and English-speaking staff. Vegetarians are well taken care of in the restaurant. ⓐ 13235 Shibokusa, Oshinomura, Minami-Tsuru-gun, Yamanashi-ken 401-105 ⓣ 05 5584 3359

Hotel Mount Fuji ££ Great views, spacious rooms and a wealth of amenities (including an ice-skating rink) make this the best property to choose in the area. Go during the week to save as much as 30 per cent off the standard rate. ⓐ 1360-83 Yamanaka, Yamanaka-ko-mura, Yamanashi-ken 403-0017 ⓣ 05 5562 2111

Mount Fuji, one of the world's most beautiful sights

HAKONE

Hot springs and views are the two huge draws of this resort area located close to Mount Fuji. It's a popular day trip for stressed-out city dwellers. Try to avoid it during summer weekends when the traffic and crowds can cancel out any of the restorative benefits. The standard trail goes from Odawara by train to Togendai through spectacular mountain passes.

Hakone-machi Tourist Association ⓐ 698 Yumoto, Hakone-machi ⓣ 04 605 8911

GETTING THERE

Take one of the frequent trains from Shinjuku to Odawara. For the best views, splurge for seats in the Romance Car, which offers comfortable seating and observation windows.

SIGHTS & ATTRACTIONS

Hakone Barrier

In the days when Kyoto was the location for the Imperial Court and Edo the home of the shogunate, the only road between the two passed straight through Hakone. Wanting to monitor the flow of people between the two, the shogunate built this barrier as an early form of traffic camera in order to keep track of who was doing what and where they were going.

One of the most important functions of the barrier was as an imprisoning gate for female nobles. The shoguns were constantly paranoid about uprisings and power struggles. In order to keep the nobility in check, they created a law that forced them to keep their wives in Edo at all times as a form of bartering chip. The theory was that if they even thought about trying to rebel, they would quickly back down if their beloved women were imprisoned. The structure standing today is not the original – it is a replica constructed in 1965. Go inside to see the collection of weapons and costumes taken from its peak years of importance.

Ⓐ Ichiban-cho, Hakone-machi Ⓣ 04 603 6635 Ⓛ 09.00–16.30 Mar–Nov, 09.00–16.00 Dec–Feb. Admission charge.

'Pirate' ships give trips on the lake at Hakone

Owaku-dani

This valley of volcanic rock showcases the power of the Earth's volcanic activity. Steam vents billowing sulphurous smoke waft all over the area – viewable from the gondola that departs regularly from Soun-zan. After you reach your terminus, enjoy the 75 m (246 ft) trail which takes you through the desolate landscape, past the ominous steam vents.

CULTURE

Hakone Museum of Art and Soun-zan (Mount Soun)

Take the cable-car from the nondescript town of Gora up Mount Soun to enjoy the views from the top. An art museum chronicling the ceramics of East Asia is located at the second stop from the bottom. While it isn't a must-do, it's enjoyable for fans of porcelain and pots.

ⓐ 1300 Gora ⓣ 04 602 2623 ⓛ 09.30–16.30 Fri–Wed, Apr–Nov, 09.30–16.00 Fri–Wed, Dec–Mar. Admission charge.

Hakone Open-Air Museum

This brilliant collection of sculpture is notable not only for the quality of the works, but also for its breathtaking location. See examples from the hands of both Japanese and Western artists, including Giacometti, Rodin and Henry Moore.

ⓐ 1121 Mi-no-taira ⓣ 04 602 1161 ⓦ www.hakone-oam.or.jp ⓛ 09.00–17.00 Mar–Nov, 09.00–16.00 Dec–Feb. Admission charge.

AFTER DARK

The Hakone region is popular due to the serenity of the area and opportunities for relaxation. As such, there isn't much of a drinking and party scene. Most visitors stick close to their hotels for the evening on a half-board basis. Local restaurants are pretty much all the same. Here, it's more about the views than about the stomach. If you do decide to eat out, you'll pay through the nose for the privilege. Pack a picnic for the day and tuck into the evening meal provided at your accommodation.

ACCOMMODATION

Fuji-Hakone Guest House £ English-speaking, family-run guest house with simple tatami rooms. Find your way there by taking the bus from Odawara station and ask for the Senkyoro-mae stop. ⓐ 912 Sengoku-hara, Hakone, Kanagawa-ken 250-0631 ⓣ 04 604 6577

Fujiya Hotel ££–£££ The Fujiya is an institution in these parts. Constructed in the Western style, it provides Japanese service making for a delightfully quirky mix of two cultures. While the rooms could do with some renovation these days, the bathrooms are highly recommended as local hot-spring water is pumped directly into the bathtubs. ⓐ 359 Miyanoshita, Hakone-machi, Kanagawa-ken 250-0522 ⓣ 04 602 2211 ⓦ www.fujiyahotel.co.jp

Yokohama

Often overshadowed by its much larger neighbour, Japan's second-largest city is a destination in its own right thanks to huge financial investment in the region's infrastructure and attractions. Located just across the bay from Tokyo, Yokohama has long had a reputation as a suburb of the capital – but this reputation is slowly being dispelled as the city centre develops independently from its larger neighbour.

Just over 150 years ago, Yokohama was a whisper of a fishing village. But that changed with the arrival of Commodore Matthew Perry, who selected the hamlet as the site of the first Japanese port to be opened to foreign trade since the Tokugawa shogunate adopted a policy of national isolation in 1639.

Just across the bay from Tokyo, Yokohama is one of Japan's chief ports

The economy, boosted by the arrival of hundreds of foreign merchants and traders, began to boom – and the good times continued with the installation of a rail link between the city and Tokyo in 1872.

Today, Yokohama is a thriving industrial centre with a slew of top-notch museums and redevelopment projects. The waterfront is especially fascinating.

Yokohama Convention & Visitors Bureau Ⓐ Yokohama Station, 2-16-1 Takashima, Nishi-ku Ⓣ 04 5441 7300 Ⓦ www.welcome.city.yokohama.jp/eng/tourism Ⓛ 09.00–19.00 Ⓜ Metro: Yokohama

GETTING THERE

Take the super-express train from Tokyo's Shibuya station to Yokohama. Total journey time is 27 minutes. Bullet trains from Tokyo station take 15 minutes but are much more expensive.

SIGHTS & ATTRACTIONS

International Stadium Yokohama

The final match of the 2002 World Cup between Germany and Brazil took place in this stadium. Visitors can relive the passion by touring the untouched dressing rooms of both teams and running onto the pitch as the World Cup anthem bellows through the stands. Ⓐ 3300 Kozukue-cho, Kohoku-ku Ⓣ 04 5477 5000 Ⓛ Tours when stadium not in use: 10.30, 12.00, 13.30 & 15.00 daily Ⓜ Metro: Shin-Yokohama. Admission charge.

Landmark Tower

Truly the symbol of Tokyo, the Landmark Tower is the tallest skyscraper in Japan. Boasting the world's fastest lift at 45 kph (28 mph), the building offers spectacular views of Tokyo and Mount Fuji.

ⓐ 2-2-1-1 Minato Mirai, Nishi-Ku ⓣ 04 5222 5035 ⓦ www.landmark.ne.jp ⓛ 10.00–22.00 daily in summer, 10.00–21.00 Mon–Fri, Sun, 10.00–22.00 Sat rest of year ⓜ Metro: Minato Mirai. Admission charge.

Marine Tower

When this tower was built in the early 1960s, it was a symbol of the rebirth of Japan following the ravages of World War II. Today, it is far from architecturally interesting, and at only 106 m (348 ft) there are plenty of higher skyscrapers. A navigational beacon near the peak of the building allows it to be classified as one of the largest lighthouses in the world.

ⓐ 15 Yamashita-cho, Naka-ku ⓣ 04 5641 7838 ⓦ www.hmk.co.jp ⓛ 09.30–19.00 Jan & Feb, 09.30–21.00 Mar–Dec ⓜ Metro: Motomachi-Chukagai. Admission charge.

Minato-no-Mieru Oka Koen (Harbour View Park)

After Yokohama was opened to foreigners, the area around what is now known as Harbour View Park was selected as the residential district for Westerners. The buildings that surround the park are reminiscent of a great European capital complete with mansions, places of worship and private schools. It remains the prime place of residence in the city today. The actual park is of interest mostly for historical reasons. Go to the rose garden

The Yokohama Landmark Tower was built to be earthquake resistant

just inside the gates to spot the building that housed the first British consulate in Japan.
ⓐ 114 Yamate-cho, Naka-ku ⓣ 04 5622 8244
ⓦ www.hamaspo.com/stadium Park open 24 hours daily, Museum hours vary Metro: Motomachi-Chukagai. Admission charge for Memorial Museum only.

Sankei-en

Probably one of Japan's most beautiful gardens, Sankei-en was planned in 1906 by a local silk merchant. Cherry blossom season (see page 14) is the best time to witness the beauty of the flowers as they drape over the various pagodas and pathways.
ⓐ 58-1 Hommoku-Sannotani, Naka-ku ⓣ 04 5621 0635
ⓦ www.sankeien.or.jp 09.00–16.30 daily Metro: Yokohama, then bus 8 or 125 to Honmoku Sankeien-mae

Yamashita Koen (Yamashita Park)

This large park owes much to the Great Kanto Earthquake of 1923. Before that horrible incident, this region was covered in warehouses and factories which were destroyed and swept away by the waves that crashed ashore along the waterfront. Inside the park is a 1930s ocean liner by the name of *Hikawa Maru*, a legendary ship that plied the seas between Yokohama and Seattle for decades. It remains preserved in its original splendour. Silent screen star Charlie Chaplin once travelled in one of the cabins and his room remains untouched (complete with some of his selected furnishings and accessories).
ⓐ Yamashita-cho, Naka-ku ⓣ 04 5641 4362 ⓦ www.hmk.co.jp

Park open 24 hours daily, *Hikawa Maru* hours vary Metro: Motomachi-Chukagai. Admission charge for *Hikawa Maru* only.

Yokohama Cosmoworld

With only 30 or so rides and attractions on offer, this amusement park isn't exactly large – but it does boast the world's biggest water-chute ride. The Ferris wheel in the centre of the park with the digital clock is considered a local landmark, especially for courting couples. At more than 112 m (367 ft) in height, it's also up there in terms of size.

2-8-1 Shinkou, Naka-ku 04 5641 6591 www.senyo.co.jp/cosmo 11.00–21.00 Mon–Fri, 11.00–22.00 Sat & Sun, Mar–Nov; 11.00–20.00 Mon–Fri, 11.00–21.00 Sat & Sun, Dec–Feb Metro: Minato Mirai

CULTURE

Silk Museum

During its peak trading years, Yokohama was the silk capital of Japan. This museum chronicles the period and provides examples of fine fabrics and a chronicle of the silk making process.

1 Yamashita-cho, Naka-ku 04 5641 0841 09.00–16.00 Tues–Sun Metro: Motomachi-Chukagai. Admission charge.

Yamate Museum

Find out more about the early years of foreign settlement in Japan in this Western building that takes a look at Western influences in the city.

Ⓐ 247 Yamate-cho, Naka-ku Ⓣ 04 5622 1188 Ⓛ 11.00–16.00
Ⓜ Metro: Motomachi-Chukagai. Admission charge.

Yokohama Doll Museum

In Japan, dolls are rarely played with. Instead, they are displayed and given spiritual and religious importance. This museum showcases almost 10,000 dolls from more than 140 countries around the world. To many locals, it is like a trip to the United Nations, with each doll acting as a high commissioner or ambassador for their nation.

Ⓐ 18 Yamashita-cho, Naka-ku Ⓣ 04 5671 9361 Ⓛ 10.00–18.00. Closed 3rd Mon of every month Ⓜ Metro: Motomachi-Chukagai. Admission charge.

Yokohama Museum of Art

If you had to choose just one sight in Yokohama, then make it this one. Considered one of the finest collections in the country, the revolving exhibitions select from the best of Western and Eastern art – both ancient and modern. The architecture itself is worth a visit.

Ⓐ 3-4-1 Minato-Mirai, Nishi-ku Ⓣ 04 5221 0300
Ⓦ www.yma.city.yokohama.jp Ⓛ 10.00–18.00 Mon–Wed, Fri–Sun
Ⓜ Metro: Minato Mirai. Admission charge.

RETAIL THERAPY

Shopping streets & districts

Basha-michi The English translation of this street is 'horse-carriage', and that's because the original lane had to be widened

The ever-colourful sights and smells of Chinatown

to accommodate the carriages Western residents imported in order to get around the city. While the street has been restored to its 19th-century splendour complete with gas lamps and antique post boxes, it can feel a bit fake. Despite this, it's a great place if you want an elegant afternoon coffee or chic souvenir shopping. ⓐ Naka-ku Ⓜ Metro: Kannai

Chinatown Yokohama has a rich tradition of welcoming Chinese immigrants to work its ports and trade its goods. The Chinatown in this city is the largest in the country and draws more than 18 million visitors a year. The streets are packed with spice shops, trinket merchants, exotic goods and anything else that could possibly have ever been made or produced in the People's Republic. For a cheap bite and even cheaper window shopping, then this is the district to head for. ⓐ Naka-ku Ⓜ Metro: Kannai

Moto-machi Yokohama's version of Fifth Avenue, Bond Street and the Champs-Élysées rolled into one – although a lot smaller! For the biggest designers, best fashions and most cutting-edge treats, then this is the place to go. As the street is pedestrianised and located close to a canal, it's a pleasant stroll regardless of the size of your wallet. ⓐ Naka-ku Ⓜ Metro: Motomachi-Chukagai

TAKING A BREAK

Shin-Yokohama Ramen Museum £ Combine culture with cuisine at this establishment which chronicles the history and importance of the humble noodle. Cheap and filling! 2-14-21 Shin-Yokohama, Kohoko-ku 04 5471 0503 www.raumen.co.jp 11.00–23.00 Mon–Fri, 10.30–23.00 Sat & Sun Metro: Shin-Yokohama

AFTER DARK

Restaurants

Manchinro Honten ££ For Japan's best Chinese food, head to the oldest restaurant in Japan's largest Chinatown. The latest incarnation of the establishment is easily the most opulent of all the eateries in the community. 153 Yamashita-cho, Naka-ku 04 5681 4004 www.manchinro.co.jp 11.00–22.00 Metro: Ishikawa-cho

Pas à Pas ££ The French treasure Japanese food. So what do the Japanese covet? French food, of course! And this is one of the better eateries in which to enjoy dishes inspired by La Belle France. Come at lunchtime for the pâtisserie and quiches. 1-50 Motomachi, Naka-ku 04 5651 5070 11.00–21.00 Tues–Sun Metro: Motomachi-Chukagai

Saronikos ££ Greek food in Japan? Strangely yes. Yokohama's long history as a port draws thousands of Greek sailors to the city – and they head straight to this restaurant for the authentic dishes and *bouzouki* music. Akebono-cho, Naka-ku 04 5251 8980 18.00–01.00 Metro: Kannai

Aichiya £££ If you like the prospect of taking your life into your hands, then this restaurant will fit the bill: fugu (a variety of blowfish that can instantly kill the eater if it hasn't been perfectly prepared) is on the menu. ⓐ 7-156 Isezaki-cho, Naka-ku ⓣ 04 5251 4163 ⓑ 15.00–22.00 ⓜ Metro: Isezaki-Choja-machi

Bars, clubs & discos

The Green Sheep Yokohama's latest Irish-themed drinking den is a firm favourite among the expat crowd. ⓐ 2-10-13 Minami-Sawai, Nishi-ku ⓣ 04 5321 0950 ⓑ 11.00–02.00 Mon–Thur, 11.00–04.00 Fri & Sat ⓜ Metro: Yokohama

ACCOMMODATION

While there *are* hotels in Yokohama, the fact that it is located just 20 minutes from Tokyo leads most visitors to stay in the capital. What properties there are gear themselves heavily to business travellers staying for day trips. If you plan on visiting frequently, select a hotel in Tokyo's Shibuya quarter for maximum convenience.

For child-specific entertainments see page 134

PRACTICAL information

Directory

GETTING THERE

By air

There are two international airports that service Tokyo: Narita and Haneda. Haneda is the more convenient by far, but primarily serves domestic flights. International service is offered to Asian and Pacific destinations via charter airlines. The Tokyo monorail links Haneda to the Tokyo metro system with a service to the city every 5–10 minutes for around ¥470.

Almost every major airline uses Narita as its Japanese gateway. Located 70 km (43 miles) from the city centre, it's a highly inconvenient airport. Arrive during rush hour and it could feel like your journey into town has taken almost as long as your flight. The easiest way to reach Tokyo is to use the Narita Express train – although you'll have to pay for the privilege. Seat reservations are a must, so peak times may see you waiting until one is available. Trains depart every 30 minutes and currently cost ¥2,940 one-way to Tokyo station.

A more affordable train option is the Keisei service. Choose from the Skyliner (60 minutes) or limited express (75 minutes), which both go to Ueno station. Tickets cost from ¥1,000–¥1,920 one-way.

Cheaper still are the limousine buses, a shared ride service that stops at major points throughout the city. Purchase your ticket at the counters on the arrivals level near the terminal exits. One-way tickets cost ¥3,000.

Whatever you do, don't even think about taking a taxi. The fare is likely to cost an extortionate ¥30,000.

Narita Express ⓣ 03 3423 0111 ⓦ www.narita-airport.or.jp
Keisei Skyliner ⓣ 04 7632 8505 ⓦ www.keisei.co.jp
Limousine bus ⓣ 03 3665 7220 ⓦ www.limousinebus.co.jp

Climate care

Many people are aware that air travel emits CO_2, which contributes to climate change. You may be interested in the possibility of lessening the environmental impact of your flight through the charity Climate Care, which offsets your CO_2 by funding environmental projects around the world. Visit ⓦ www.climatecare.org

By rail

Japan Railways is world-renowned for its speed and efficiency – although it does come at a cost. Riding a *Shinkansen* (bullet train) is an experience that must be tried at least once in life. There's nothing quite like travelling through the Japanese countryside past Mount Fuji at 270 km (168 miles) an hour. During rush hour, trains can get packed – so much so that employees are hired for the sole purpose of pushing people into the carriages. Seats are usually only available by reserving in advance, which comes at an extra cost.

Thomas Cook Overseas Timetable ⓦ www.thomascook publishing.com
Japan Railways ⓦ www.jreast.co.jp/e

By bus

Long-distance buses connect Tokyo with most other Japanese

cities. Travel costs are much reduced compared to airline and train tickets. Many departures leave cities late at night in order to reach Tokyo during the early morning hours. This is planned specifically to ensure that the journey time is not affected by heavy traffic. The long-distance train companies also run coach services, so you will find that buses depart outside the main train station of your departure point.

By road

The highway system in Japan is extremely modern and efficient. Unfortunately, there are a number of obstacles you will need to overcome if you plan to drive. The first challenge is the language barrier. While signs are in English they aren't all that descriptive, so you may find that an arrow pointing towards Tokyo is not the

As is their reputation, trains are fast, efficient and very crowded

fastest way of getting where you want to go. Second, parking is extortionate. If you are staying at a hotel, try to find one that offers parking as part of the nightly room rate or you will face a hefty bill. If the above information doesn't dissuade you from attempting to get behind the wheel, please note that you will require an international driving licence and at least six months' experience as a driver.

ENTRY FORMALITIES

Visitors to Japan who are citizens of the UK may stay in the country for up to six months without a visa. Canadian citizens may stay for up to three months. Those from the USA, Australia and New Zealand are given 90 days visa-free. All other nationalities should check with the Japanese Embassy in their home nation before departing.

Customs

Most personal effects and the following items are duty-free: 400 cigarettes or 100 cigars or 500 g of smoking tobacco, three 760 ml bottles of alcohol, two ounces of perfume and other goods up to a value of ¥100,000. There are strict restrictions against the importation of pornography, firearms and narcotics. Those caught violating regulations can face detainment, deportation or even complete refusal of entry for life.

MONEY

The currency in Japan is the yen (¥). Bill denominations are: ¥10,000, ¥5,000, ¥2,000 and ¥1,000. Coins are available in denominations of ¥500, ¥100, ¥50, ¥10, ¥5 and ¥1.

You can withdraw money using ATMs at almost all US banks. Credit cards are widely accepted for almost all transactions, with Visa and MasterCard the most commonly used. American Express is not taken by some shops and services.

HEALTH, SAFETY & CRIME

It is not necessary to take any special health precautions while travelling in Japan. Tap water is safe to drink, but many locals prefer bottled varieties and there are vending machines on almost every corner – many selling vitamin, mineral and electrolyte-enriched varieties.

Pharmacies are located throughout the city, although none are open 24 hours. If you need specific medication or require something in an emergency, go straight to the nearest hospital.

Japanese health care is of an excellent standard, but it is extremely expensive. A minor ailment requiring an overnight stay could result in expenses of thousands of dollars. As such, make sure you take out travel insurance prior to departure.

Crime in Tokyo is almost unheard of. In fact, it is commonly ranked as the safest tourist destination in the world. About the only thing you may encounter is pickpocketing, but this is so rare it's almost pointless mentioning. In the event that you are a victim, contact the police on their English-language emergency number 110. For details of additional contact numbers, refer to the 'Emergencies' section on page 138.

OPENING HOURS

Most banks and currency exchanges open Mon–Fri 09.00–15.00, although some major branches stay open for an additional hour or two. Businesses and offices are open 09.00–17.00 weekdays and Saturday mornings, so if you are in town for work, you may be expected to go in for a meeting at the weekend.

Cultural institutions are usually open from 09.00–18.00 every day except Monday. Other exceptions include the day following national holidays, New Year week and the day after a major temporary exhibit closes when maintenance staff use the time to redo the gallery.

Shops open 10.00–11.00 and stay open until 19.00–20.00 every day of the week. Department stores also remain open during these hours but will close one day during the week. The day of closure varies from store to store.

There are many 24-hour convenience stores with in-shop ATMs.

TOILETS

Thankfully, public toilets are available throughout the city. When in need, head straight for the nearest train or metro station where you are bound to find facilities either near or just inside the main entrance. Station toilets are the Japanese squat variety and don't usually offer toilet paper. Come prepared with your own stash. If you prefer Western-style facilities, then department stores offer the most comfortable option.

CHILDREN

Japan's birth rate is extremely low, which means that the sight of a child is increasingly rare – especially in the big city. As such, children are treated like gold in Tokyo. That said, they will be expected to behave. Tantrums and screaming cause major embarrassment for the Japanese who will not know how to cope with such displays of emotion. Also breast-feeding in public is decidedly frowned on. Avoid the metro or bus during the rush hour when crowds can be overwhelming. A journey is free for children under six, while under-12s pay half-price.

Below are three places to consider taking the tots to when they get bored.

Tokyo Disney Resort The Japanese branch of the park that Disney built is actually two attractions in one: Disneyland® and DisneySea®. Tokyo Disneyland® is very similar to its Los Angeles and Orlando counterparts, while DisneySea® is a water-themed amusement land with aquariums and rides dedicated to the wonders under the sea. ⓐ 1-1 Maihana, Urayasu-shi, Chiba ⓣ 04 5683 3333 ⓦ www.tokyodisneyresort.co.jp ◷ Varies Metro: Maihama. Admission charge.

National Children's Castle Five floors of toys, games and play areas designed to challenge, educate and delight. Special faves include the fourth-floor music hall (not recommended if you have a headache) and the fifth-floor roof garden with its outdoor gym and ballrooms. ⓐ 5-53-1 Jingumae, Shibuya-ku ⓣ 03 3797 5666 ⓦ www.kodomono-shiro.or.jp ◷ 12.30–17.30 Tues–Fri, 10.00–17.30 Sat & Sun Metro: Shibuya or Omotesando. Admission charge.

Koganei Park Rent a bike or tricycle, slide down the artificial hills or just stroll through this massive park, which is always a hit with families in western Tokyo. ⓐ 1-13-1 Sekino-machi, Koganei-shi ⓣ 04 2385 5611 ⓦ www.tokyo-park.or.jp/english ◷ 24-hr daily Metro: Musashi Koganei

COMMUNICATIONS

Phones

Coin and card-operated public phones are available. Local calls cost ¥10 for the first 3 minutes and ¥10 for each additional minute.

The international dialling code for calls from Japan to the UK is +44, to the Irish Republic +353, to South Africa +27, to Australia +61, to New Zealand +64, and to Canada and the United States +1.

Children will love a day at Tokyo Disneyland®

Post

Postal services are quick and efficient. Stamps can be bought at post offices or from most convenience stores. Post boxes are red – use the left slot for domestic post and the right for international. Postcards abroad cost ¥70, while letters under 25 g cost ¥90 to Asia, ¥110 to North America, Europe and Oceania, or ¥130 to Africa and South America.

Internet

Internet access is provided by most hotels and in many coffee shops; 24-hour services are also available in branches of Kinkos, which has stations throughout the city.

ELECTRICITY

The standard electrical current is 100 volts AC. Two-pin adaptors can be purchased at most electrical shops and will be required for all European appliances.

TRAVELLERS WITH DISABILITIES

Facilities for visitors with disabilities are generally quite poor in Japan. If you have mobility issues or use a wheelchair, you will find that public transport is almost impossible to use. Many stations are littered with staircases – if you need help, station staff will be more than eager to assist. Before you depart check out Accessible Tokyo (ⓦ http://accessible.jp.org) and Club Tourism (ⓦ www.club-t.com), which organises special tours designed specifically for visitors with various disabilities.

FURTHER INFORMATION

The Japan National Tourist Organisation (JNTO) is the tourist board for the country; the Tokyo Convention and Visitors Bureau (TCVB) has information on the city only, and there is a Tokyo Tourist Information Centre, which is run by the Tokyo Metropolitan Government. All offices offer maps and brochures to the main sights.

Tokyo JNTO ⓐ Tokyo Kotsu Kaikan 10th Floor, 2-10-1 Yurakucho, Chiyoda-ku ⓣ 03 3201 3331 ⓦ www.jnto.go.jp ◷ 09.00–17.00 daily Metro: Yurakucho

TCVB Information Centre ⓐ Tokyo Chamber of Commerce & Industry Building, 1st Floor, 3-2-2 Marunouchi, Chiyoda-ku ⓣ 03 3287 7024 ⓦ www.tcvb.or.jp ◷ 10.00–17.00 Mon–Fri, 10.00–16.00 Sat & Sun Metro: Yurakucho

Tokyo Tourist Information Centre ⓐ Tokyo Metropolitan Government Building No. 1, 1st Floor, 2-8-1 Nishi-Shinjuku, Shinjuku-ku ⓣ 03 5321 3077 ⓦ www.kanko.metro.tokyo.jp ◷ 09.30–18.30 daily Metro: Tochomae

BACKGROUND READING

Norwegian Wood by Haruki Murakami. Probably the most famous contemporary Japanese novelist. Most of his works are set in the streets of Tokyo.
Snow Country by Yasuwari Kawabata. Japan's first Nobel-prize winner for literature.
Hirohito and the Making of Modern Japan by Herbert P Bix. Tokyo's 20th-century history in one great read.

Emergencies

EMERGENCY NUMBERS

Ambulance 119

Police 110

Fire brigade 119

When ringing any of the above numbers on a public phone, press the red button first to ensure the person who answers speaks English.

Health

Ensure that you have private travel insurance, as health care in Japan can be expensive. For emergencies, go directly to the emergency departments of the main public hospitals.

Pharmacies are located throughout the city and generally have extended hours. Prescription and non-prescription drugs are only sold at pharmacies. Many Western medicines are forbidden by Japanese law. However, staff will try and find a suitable alternative.

Hospitals and clinics

St Luke's International Hospital 9-1 Akashicho, Chuo-ku 03 3541 5151 www.luke.or.jp Metro: Tsukiji

Tokyo Medical & Surgical Clinic Mori Building 32, 2nd Floor, 3-4-30 Shiba-koen, Minato-ku 03 3436 3028 www.tmsc.jp Metro: Shiba-koen

Police

In the event that you require police assistance, call the Metropolitan Police English-speaking service on 03 3501 0110.

Lost property

If you lose something, you will most likely find it tucked away safely by the owner of the establishment you left it in. Items left in public transport stations should be tracked down at the stationmaster's office. Failing that, look for a police box and ask for someone who speaks English.

Consulates & embassies

Australian Embassy ⓐ 2-1-14 Mita, Minato-ku ⓣ 03 5232 4111 ⓦ www.australia.jp Metro: Azabu-Juban

British Embassy ⓐ 1 Ichibansho, Chiyoda-ku ⓣ 03 5211 1100 ⓦ www.uknow.or.jp Metro: Hanzomon

Canadian Embassy ⓐ 7-3-38 Akasaka, Minato-ku ⓣ 03 5412 6200 ⓦ www.canadanet.or.jp Metro: Aoyama-Itchome

Irish Embassy ⓐ 2-10-7 Kojimachi, Chiyoda-ku ⓣ 03 3263 0695 ⓦ www.embassy-avenue.jp Metro: Hanzomon

New Zealand Embassy ⓐ 20-40 Kamiyamacho, Shibuya-ku ⓣ 03 3467 2271 ⓦ www.nzembassy.com Metro: Yoyogi-Koen

South African Embassy ⓐ Zenkyoren Building, 4th Floor, 2-7-9 Hirakawacho, Chiyoda-ku ⓣ 03 3265 3366 ⓦ www.ratsk.com Metro: Nagatacho

US Embassy ⓐ 1-10-5 Akasaka, Minato-ku ⓣ 03 3224 5000 ⓦ http://tokyo.usembassy.gov Metro: Tameike-Sanno

INDEX

The publishers would like to thank Mark Bassett/The Source for providing all the photographs in this book, with the exception of: page 26 (Pictures Colour Library); pages 17, 21, 89, 113, 116 and 135 (World Pictures); page 18 (© Photographer: Galina Barskaya/ Agency:Dreamstime.com).

Copy editor: Sandra Stafford
Proofreader: Amanda Jones

Send your thoughts to
books@thomascook.com

- **Found a great bar, club, shop or must-see sight that we don't feature?**
- **Like to tip us off about any information that needs updating?**
- **Want to tell us what you love about this handy little guidebook and more importantly how we can make it even handier?**

Then here's your chance to tell all! Send us ideas, discoveries and recommendations today and then look out for your valuable input in the next edition of this title.

Send an email to the above address (stating the book's title) or write to: CitySpots Project Editor, Thomas Cook Publishing, PO Box 227, The Thomas Cook Business Park, Coningsby Road, Peterborough PE3 8SB, UK.